Emotional Intelligence for a Compassionate World

Workbook for Enhancing Emotional Intelligence Skills

Barbara A. Kerr PhD

ISBN-13: 9781544607665
ISBN-10: 1544607660
Library of Congress Control Number: 2017905126
CreateSpace Independent Publishing Platform
North Charleston, South Carolina

Emotional Intelligence for a Compassionate World

Acknowledgements

Emotional Intelligence for a Compassionate World began as an online course offered as part of the curriculum of the Compassion Education Institute, in partnership with the Charter for Compassion International. It has been my pleasure and privilege to engage with hundreds of students with whom I interacted both in person and online. Students asked to have the information and links in a book format so they could review what they had learned or look back at suggestions for improving their Emotional Intelligence skills. I am grateful to those many students who participated in the course over the years—in the live version as well as the online edition. Their comments, insights, suggestions, and questions have enriched my understanding, broadened my horizons, and often made their way into this book.

I owe a debt of gratitude to Mary O'Neill, who incorporated many of the exercises in her live workshops, and Patrick McLaughlin who reviewed an early version of the course. I am grateful, as well, to the team at the Compassion Education Institute: Olivia McIvor, Debra Scholten, and Kelley Haynes-Mendez for their intelligence and organizational skills—but mostly for their kindness always. I would especially like to acknowledge the help and unfailing support of Don Rooks and Lisa Davis, who have graciously edited the materials in the course and now the book, and who have provided encouragement at every step—the wind beneath my wings.

What to Expect

The information, the activities, and the assignments that make up *Emotional Intelligence for a Compassionate World* will lead you on a journey to discover answers to your questions, to satisfy your curiosity, and to assist you in building your skills for greater personal satisfaction and success in your relationships at home, in the workplace, and in the wider world.

The opening chapter provides an overview of Emotional Intelligence and introduces the Success Model. The following five chapters go into more detail about each of the five dimensions of that model: Awareness of the Self, Actions of the Self, Awareness of Others, Interaction with Others, and Resilience. Each chapter also includes activities for you to practice and improve skills, and each concludes with a reflection as well as suggestions for further enhancement.

The final chapter includes two planning guides. One is an Action Plan for Emotional Intelligence—an opportunity for you to commit to actions for improvement. In addition, you will find a Compassionate Action Plan, which will guide you in taking steps toward being more compassionate. Enjoy the journey!

In this workbook, you'll have access to plenty of information, but you will be working toward several specific learning outcomes.

- You will connect EI skills to the development of self-compassion, compassion for others, and global compassion.
- You will become more aware of the role that emotions play in everyday experience, in both the personal and professional aspects of your life.
- You will be better able to identify your own emotions and plan how to manage them.
- You will learn techniques to become more adept at reading emotional cues in others to build productive teams and support networks.
- You will be more able to positively influence others by changing the way you interact with them.
- You will become more aware of the importance of building and maintaining your resilience despite the stresses that are part of any workplace and an inevitable aspect of all our lives.
- You will also have the opportunity to create an Action Plan for improving your own EI skills and to complete a Plan for Compassionate Action.

Contents

One

An Introduction to
Emotional Intelligence

WHY EMOTIONAL INTELLIGENCE?

Emotions are a constant in the lives of us humans. Everyday. Everywhere. No matter who we are, where we live, or what we do, Emotions color our moments, our days, our years, and our entire lives.

While there are people who suffer from brain diseases or have had an injury to the brain, most of us feel the ups and downs of our human emotions. We do the best we can not only to deal with those emotions but also to navigate through the minefields of other people's emotions every day.

By the time we have completed the years of childhood and adolescence, we are expected to have mastered this aspect of our lives, to demonstrate by our behaviors that we are the masters of our emotions. But is that true?

Why then do we so often pretend that we are not feeling an emotion?

Why do we attempt to hide our emotions from others?

Why do we feel that we must "park our emotions at the door?"

Why is it that we often have difficulty figuring out what it is we are feeling?

Why are we sometimes frightened or surprised by feeling an emotion?

Why do we so often have difficulty managing those strong emotions—jealousy, loneliness, anger for example?

How do we remain calm and caring or supportive while others are experiencing these strong emotions?

How is it possible for us to increase the emotions we would like to have more of, such as compassion or kindness?

And why is it that some people seem to be able to handle their emotions better than others?

These questions are all part of the topic of Emotional Intelligence.

WHAT DOES IT MEAN TO BE EMOTIONALLY INTELLIGENT?

In the growing body of research about Emotional Intelligence, which now includes studies in the fields of neuroscience and positive psychology, an increasing number of definitions, assessments, and models have been offered. Let's hit a few of the highlights.

Reuven Bar-On, an American-born Israeli clinical psychologist, developed one of the first and now most well-validated assessment instruments, the EQ-i. Bar-On focused his research by asking a couple of questions:

- Why do some people succeed in possessing better emotional well-being than others?
- Why are some individuals more able to succeed in life than others?

"Emotional intelligence is concerned with effectively understanding oneself and others, relating well to people, and adapting to and coping with the immediate surroundings to be more successful in dealing with environmental demands."

---REUVEN BAR-ON

Salovey and Mayer (at Yale University and the University of New Hampshire) coined the term "emotional intelligence" in the 1990's, initiating a research program on non-cognitive aspects of intelligence to measure EI and explore their significance.

"[Emotional Intelligence is] the ability to monitor one's own and others' feelings and emotions, to discriminate among them and to use this information to guide one's thinking and actions."

--PETER SALOVEY AND JOHN D. MAYER

Daniel Goleman received a doctorate from Harvard and is an internationally known psychologist who served as a science journalist reporting on the brain and behavioral sciences for *The New York Times* for many years.

"[Emotional Intelligence is] the capacity for recognizing our own feelings and those of others, for motivating ourselves, and for managing emotions well in ourselves and in our relationships."

--DANIEL GOLEMAN

Josh Freedman has developed his own model and global training program called Six Seconds (see 6seconds.org), an international non-profit whose mission is to support people to create positive change by increasing Emotional Intelligence.

"Know Yourself. Choose Yourself. Give Yourself"

"Emotions make or break relationships, they lead us to optimal or terrible decisions, they drive our best and worst behaviors . . . the difference is emotional intelligence."

--JOSH FREEDMAN

This definition is from Robert Cooper and Ayman Sawaf, authors of *Executive EQ: Emotional Intelligence in Leadership and Organizations* (1997).

"Emotional intelligence is the ability to sense, understand, and effectively apply the power and acumen of emotions as a source of human energy, information, connection, and influence."

--ROBERT COOPER AND AYMAN SAWAF

Question for Reflection: How do *you* recognize a person as emotionally intelligent?

_____

_____

_____

_____

_____

_____

GPS: A METAPHOR FOR EMOTIONAL INTELLIGENCE

For those of you who like a metaphor or an analogy to help you understand and remember an abstract concept, the GPS (global positioning system) has some interesting parallels to Emotional Intelligence. Once a high-tech system for the military and satellites, the GPS is now in common use to help people navigate in the wilderness as well as in cities and small towns all over the globe.

GPS (Global Positioning System)		EI (Emotional Intelligence)
Helps you identify your current position		What am I feeling right now?
Prompts you to identify where you want to go		What outcome do I want in this situation?
Assists with dealing with obstacles and changes in the environment as they occur		What can I do now to create the outcome I desire?
Recalculates new routes to your destination as conditions and/or your position changes—without drama or blame		How can I get back on a course that will bring satisfaction and success?
Helps you reach your intended destination despite obstacles and an altered environment		How can I learn to gracefully cope with an ever-changing environment?

Emotional intelligence can serve as your own *inner GPS* helping you navigate through the complex of emotions in yourself and in your interactions with others. During this course, we will look at examples of Emotional Intelligence in a few different settings—but the fact is that emotions and their effects are everywhere.

Question for Reflection: Keeping in mind that no analogy is perfect, does the GPS metaphor/analogy help you gain a better feel for the ways in which Emotional Intelligence can be helpful to you?

_____

_____

_____

_____

SO WHAT?

"Self-absorption in all its forms kills empathy, let alone compassion. When we focus on ourselves, our world contracts as our problems and preoccupations loom large. But when we focus on others, our world expands. Our own problems drift to the periphery of the mind and so seem smaller, and we increase our capacity for connection—or compassionate action."

--DANIEL GOLEMAN

This quote is from *Social Intelligence: The New Science of Human Relationships* by Daniel Goleman, one of the leading voices in the field of Emotional Intelligence.

We've talked a bit about the *What?* of Emotional Intelligence, and we'll consider it in more detail in a few minutes. But for now, let's consider the *"So What?"* Why has there been such a burgeoning interest—indicated by hundreds of books, articles, and studies--in Emotional Intelligence?

And more to the point--why should you care about developing or improving the skills of Emotional Intelligence? How can learning the skills of Emotional Intelligence be helpful to you—or to your team—or to your community? Or to making a difference in the world?

Question for Reflection: Take all the time you need to consider Goleman's quote and to reflect on these questions about the "So What?" of Emotional Intelligence.

_____

_____

_____

_____

_____

_____

LET'S TRY THAT . . .

Ready for a bit of an experiment?

First—make a short mental list of the problems you are experiencing in your life right now (this can be as small as an annoying hangnail or as big as worrying about a loved one who is gravely ill). Don't spend a lot of time on this—just think of a few things that are bothering you today.

Now, I'm hoping to shock or at least surprise you with a list of statistics about problems that people in our world community are experiencing. As you read through these, see if your problems get any smaller by comparison. Also—note whether you feel any empathy for the people described here—and think about whether you might be moved to actually do something to help resolve any of these problems.

(The following statistics are from The Hunger Project: http://www.thp.org/knowledge-center/know-your-world-facts-about-hunger-poverty/).

WORLD HUNGER

- **795 million people** – or one in nine people in the world – do not have enough to eat.
- **98% of the world's undernourished people** live in developing countries.

WOMEN AND CHILDREN

- **60 percent** of the world's hungry are women.
- **50 percent of pregnant women** in developing countries lack proper maternal care, resulting in approximately **300,000 maternal deaths** annually from childbirth.
- **1 out of 6** infants are born with a low birth weight in developing countries.
- Nearly half of all deaths in children under 5 are attributable to under-nutrition. This translates into the unnecessary loss of about **3 million young lives a year**.
- **Every 10 seconds,** a child dies from hunger-related diseases.

HIV/AIDS AND OTHER DISEASES

- **36.9 million people** are living with HIV/AIDS.
- **50 percent of people** living with HIV/AIDS are women.
- **88 percent of all children and 60 percent of all women** living with HIV are in sub-Saharan Africa.
- **6.3 million children died in 2013** – 17,000 a day- mostly from preventable health issues such as malaria, diarrhea and pneumonia.

POVERTY

- About **896 million people** in developing countries live on $1.90 a day or less.
- **22,000 children** die each day due to conditions of poverty.

AGRICULTURE

- **70 percent of the world's poorest people** live in rural areas and depend on agriculture and related activities for their livelihood.
- **50 percent of hungry people** are farming families.

WATER AND SANITATION

- **663 million people** lack access to clean water.
- **2.4 billion people** do not have adequate sanitation.
- **Each day, nearly 1,000 children die** due to preventable water and sanitation-related diarrhoeal diseases

Question for Reflection: Well—how did your mind-experiment work? Did becoming more aware of these problems have any effect on how you view your own problems?

_____

_____

EMOTIONAL INTELLIGENCE AND LEADERSHIP

"If your actions inspire others to dream more, learn more, do more and become more, you are a leader."

-- JOHN QUINCY ADAMS

The skills of Emotional Intelligence are a valuable and necessary aspect of sound leadership. And everyone is a potential leader whether in the family, among friends, in a group of community volunteers, or in the workplace. By becoming your best self and inspiring others to be their best selves, you are a leader.

THE "DARK SIDE" OF EMOTIONAL INTELLIGENCE

Just think for a moment about politicians and other world leaders who, throughout history, have had so much power to sway emotions—for ill as well as for good. The current global climate is full of examples of men and women who can inspire us to positive attitudes and action; unfortunately, we can also think of some leaders who influence others to violent, destructive, and hurtful actions.

Leaders lead because of the influence they have on the emotions of followers. Indeed, emotions are the *primary energy* behind anyone's leadership. The "dark side" of this concept is that leaders can manipulate others for selfish ends. The skills of Emotional Intelligence can provide an ethical leader with the ability to influence others for positive change. This can happen within a family, a non-profit community organization, a large corporation, and even an entire country.

WE RELY ON THE EMOTIONS OF OUR LEADERS

When a catastrophe occurs—a devastating hurricane, a destructive forest fire, a killer earthquake—we expect our government leaders (presidents, governors, mayors) to not only go to view those situations but to speak publicly about them. Why? We expect them to express some emotion about the situation as well as provide information about what will be done to resolve the problem.

The actions and attitudes of our leaders have great influence on how we feel about a given situation.

Resource: "Don't Eat Those Carrots! Emotional Intelligence and Ethics," http://emotionalintelligenceinsights.com/don't-eat-those-carrots-emotional-intelligence-and-ethics/

Question for Reflection: Think of a leader you are familiar with (or it could be you) in an organization or community—perhaps a place where you have worked or lived. Does this person have "power to sway everyone's emotions" when something important has occurred or when a significant decision must be made? Is the impact that the leader makes mostly positive and inspiring—or negative and destructive?

_____

_____

_____

_____

_____

_____

EMOTIONAL INTELLIGENCE, COMPASSION AND YOUR HEALTH

On a more personal basis, there are also a number of good reasons for paying attention to your Emotional Intelligence skills. For example, the quality of our relationships—which can be enhanced through Emotional Intelligence skills—can have a huge impact on our physical heath:

- Studies have shown a connection between lack of emotional support and heart disease.
- There is good evidence that relationships can either buffer or intensify illness.
- Daniel Goleman, one of the researchers and writers in the forefront of this topic, has written: "Toxic relationships are as major a risk factor for disease and death as are: smoking, high blood pressure or cholesterol, obesity, and physical inactivity."Goleman goes on to explain that cortisol is the active substance. The connection between toxic relationships and health risk is especially true of a relationship that involves criticism—especially unanswered criticism.

In addition, if the development of EI skills includes an increase in the *ability to be empathetic and compassionate*, the potential benefits to the individual are great. According to research done at The Greater Good Science Center at Berkeley, being compassionate has many benefits including the following:

- Compassion makes us feel good: Compassionate action (e.g., giving to charity) activates pleasure circuits in the brain and lead to lasting increases in self-reported happiness.
- Being compassionate—tuning in to other people in a kind and loving manner—can reduce risk of heart disease by boosting the positive effects of the Vagus Nerve, which helps to slow our heart rate.
- Compassion makes people more resilient to stress; it lowers stress hormones in the blood and saliva and strengthens the immune response.

Resource: The Greater Good Science Center: http://greatergood.berkeley.edu/topic/compassion

EMOTIONAL INTELLIGENCE AND THE WORKPLACE

"Employees who receive more compassion in their workplace see themselves, their co-workers, and their organization in a more positive light, report feeling more positive emotions like joy and contentment, and are more committed to their jobs."

—GREATER GOOD SCIENCE CENTER

Many studies have been conducted on the connection of Emotional Intelligence to:

- Kinder and more compassionate environments
- Increased morale
- Greater job satisfaction
- Deeper commitment
- Higher retention of valuable employees
- Significantly more harmony in the workplace
- Improved customer relations, customer satisfaction, work relationships and teamwork
- Better collaboration
- Increased innovation
- More successful negotiations

Question for Reflection: What might stronger EI skills accomplish in your workplace?

_____

_____

_____

_____

_____

EMOTIONAL INTELLIGENCE FOR A COMPASSIONATE WORLD

"More compassionate societies—those that take care of their most vulnerable members, assist other nations in need, and have children who perform more acts of kindness—are the happier ones."

—GREATER GOOD SCIENCE CENTER

There are wider implications of Emotional Intelligence as well. Paul Ekman is a research scientist and professor who has been a pioneer in the study of emotions and of their relation to facial expressions. He and the Dalai Lama co-authored the book, *Emotional Awareness: Overcoming the Obstacles to Psychological Balance and Compassion.*

New studies, articles, and books about Emotional Intelligence are published every day. We've included a selected reference list in the appendix to get you started if you are interested in reading more. It also includes books or articles referenced in this book.

The important message in all of this is that Emotional Intelligence is indeed related to your success—as an individual, as a team member, as a member of your organization, and your community. We believe Emotional Intelligence is also at the core for developing the empathy and compassionate action that can bring positive change to all beings and to the Earth itself.

Question for Reflection: The Dalai Lama has said, "Love and compassion are necessities, not luxuries. Without them, humanity cannot survive." What are your thoughts about compassion? Is it a necessity in your life? In your family, workplace, or community?

_____

_____

_____

_____

_____

TAKE A SELF-ASSESSMENT IN EMOTIONAL INTELLIGENCE

Before we go further to discuss the components of Emotional Intelligence, we suggest that you take and score the self-assessment below. The assessment and score are for your eyes only, so be honest as you answer the thirty items.

The assessment will provide you with a baseline indication of your own skills in five dimensions. Taking the assessment will also help frame the presentation and discussions that follow in this book.

If you've already taken an assessment, such as the EQ-i, we suggest that you also take this self-assessment because it will be useful to you as we go on to discuss in more detail the skills of Emotional Intelligence and how to enhance them for your own success.

EMOTIONAL INTELLIGENCE ASSESSMENT

Respond to each of the 30 statements with one of the following:

1 = Rarely like me

2 = Occasionally like me

3 = Sometimes like me

4 = Often like me

5 = Almost always like me

_____	1.	I know which situations and/or people are likely to make me feel frustrated or angry.
_____	2.	When I have accomplished a difficult task, I take time to appreciate my work.
_____	3.	When I write an email, I think about how the receiver will feel reading it.
_____	4.	I publicly give credit to those who help me accomplish a task or goal.
_____	5.	Even when I am disappointed with poor results, I am optimistic about working toward a better outcome.
_____	6.	When I feel angry, I am able to identify the cause.
_____	7.	When I am frustrated or angry, I remain composed.
_____	8.	I recognize when others are nervous or ill-at-ease in my presence.
_____	9.	I am open to suggestions and ideas from others even if they disagree with my ideas.
_____	10.	I view problems as interesting challenges to solve.
_____	11.	I recognize when my energy is low.
_____	12.	At the close of a meeting, I am clear about what actions I will take next.
_____	13.	When I am in a small group of family, friends, or colleagues, I attempt to understand the mood of each person
_____	14.	When the person I am with is irritated, I adjust my behavior as I work with him or her.
_____	15.	When I receive bad news, I give myself some time to absorb it and then move on.
_____	16.	When I speak, I am aware of the impact I have on others.
_____	17.	When I make a mistake, I openly admit to it.
_____	18.	I try to identify the emotions and feelings that other people may be experiencing.

_____	19.	When teaching someone to do something, I am patient if the person is slow to understand.
_____	20.	When I am feeling disappointed after working toward a goal, I am able to express my disappointment and keep working.
_____	21.	I am aware that my mood and conversation affect how others around me feel and act.
_____	22.	I observe others carefully to learn beneficial behaviors or skills.
_____	23.	If a friend, family member, or colleague shows irritation or impatience, I try to understand what he/she is feeling.
_____	24.	I welcome feedback from my friends and family.
_____	25.	I am able to adjust when there are major changes (for example, cancellation of dinner plans with friends, or changing a vacation destination).
_____	26.	When I feel sad, I can identify the cause.
_____	27.	When I am in a bad mood, I am able to remain patient with other people.
_____	28.	I try to understand how others are feeling by putting myself in their place and imagining how I would feel.
_____	29.	I encourage people to speak up if they disagree with my point of view.
_____	30.	When I am upset about a personal issue, I find it difficult to stay focused on my work.

Go on to the next page to score your assessment.

SCORING THE ASSESSMENT

Transfer your item scores to the spaces below. Then add each column.

1_____	2_____	3_____	4_____	5_____
6_____	7_____	8_____	9_____	10_____
11_____	12_____	13_____	14_____	15_____
16_____	17_____	18_____	19_____	20_____
21_____	22_____	23_____	24_____	25_____
26_____	27_____	28_____	29_____	30_____

Total _____   _____   _____   _____   _____

| Awareness Of the Self | Actions of the Self | Awareness of Others | Interaction with Others | Resilience |

Results

Plot your scores on the chart below to see whether you are "Highly Effective," "Effective," or you have "Room for Improvement."

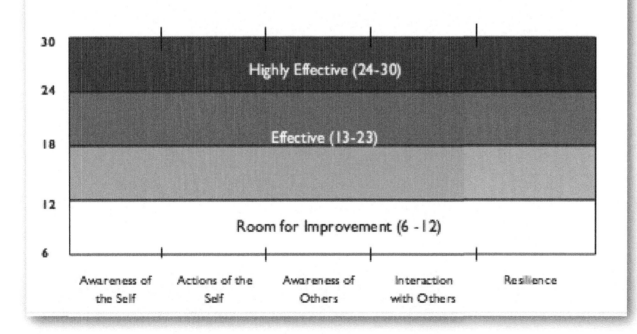

IQ AND EQ – WHAT'S THE DIFFERENCE?

Summing up what we've covered so far—there are many good reasons for paying attention to the concepts of Emotional Intelligence in our personal lives, in the workplace, and in the wider community. Let's turn now to understanding how these ideas have developed over time.

IQ, EI, EQ, ESI –WHY SO MANY OF THESE LETTERS?

You are probably already familiar with the concept of IQ or Intelligence Quotient. The idea of measuring intelligence took hold in the early part of the twentieth century. The tests place people on a bell-shaped curve with the "average" intelligence at 100.

Emotional Intelligence (EI) is now often referred to as Emotional and Social Intelligence (ESI) or, because people are familiar with IQ, as EQ or Emotional Quotient.

WHAT IS INTELLIGENCE ANYWAY?

Emotional Intelligence skills probably should have been included as part of the IQ tests. As Cary Cherniss explains in his article, "Emotional Intelligence: What it is and Why it Matters," the early developers of IQ tests understood that "non-intellective" abilities are as important for predicting an individual's success in life as those of general intelligence.

INTRAPERSONAL AND INTERPERSONAL SKILLS ARE KEY

The IQ test as we know it was developed mostly as a measure of mathematical and verbal abilities. In his book, *Frames of Mind: The Theory of Multiple Intelligences*, published in 1983, Howard Gardner wrote about multiple intelligences, including "intrapersonal" and "interpersonal" intelligences, which would later become major aspects of Emotional Intelligence definitions.

In almost every model of Emotional Intelligence, these two aspects—interpersonal and intrapersonal--are key components. Emotional Intelligence helps us navigate emotions in both our internal world and the external world.

EMOTIONAL INTELLIGENCE AND THE BRAIN

Daniel Goleman, the author of the 1995 book, *Emotional Intelligence: Why it Can Matter More than IQ*, greatly boosted popular interest in Emotional Intelligence. Goleman remains a recognized expert in this field and has written many books and articles.

In another book, *Social Intelligence: The New Science of Human Relationships* (2006), which Goleman wrote as a companion to the 1995 book, Dr. Goleman makes the case for each person having a "social brain," which connects us to all those we interact with. He says that those interactions mold both our experience and our neural circuitry.

When scientists who study the brain place people in MRI machines and present "positive" or "negative" images to them, they are able to observe brain activity in response to the stimuli. This kind of study is called an f-MRI (functional MRI). In this way they are able to study what Goleman calls the "social brain"—a sort of "social superhighway," which operates automatically as we interact with others.

Resource: You may want to visit Goleman's blog at www.danielgoleman.info to read more about the many facets of Emotional Intelligence. You might also be interested in Goleman's more recent book, *A Force for Good: The Dalai Lama's Vision for Our World,* 2015, Random House.

NEUROSCIENCE, MIRROR NEURONS, EMOTIONAL INTELLIGENCE

Even as you are reading the material in this book, your brain is laying down new neuronal pathways. Throughout your lifetime, the neurons in your brain will continue to grow in response to the new things that you learn and do. We find that to be a really exciting concept and a good image to keep in mind.

Neuroscientists are studying several systems of "mirror neurons"—neurons that reflect back an action we observe in someone else—making us mimic that action or have the impulse to do so. So for example, if you could see me opening and closing my fists, you would probably feel the impulse to so the same with your own fists. Inside your head, you are copying my actions, even if you are not actually making a fist. That is your mirror neurons at work. We're all familiar with this from watching someone else yawn. It can be difficult to keep yourself from yawning too.

Neurologist and neuroscientist Marco Iacoboni, currently at the David Geffen School of Medicine at UCLA, has written a fascinating book, *Mirroring People—the New Science of How We Connect with Others*. Through simulation experiments and brain mapping, Iacoboni has learned much about the communication of emotions.

His experiments have led him to say:

> *"It seems as if our brain is built for mirroring, and that only through mirroring . . . do we deeply understand what other people are feeling."*

Understanding what other people are feeling is an important aspect of Emotional Intelligence—and a skill you can improve. The ability to empathize, to feel what another person feels even in a situation you have never experienced, is a crucial step toward becoming more compassionate and building meaningful, satisfying relationships with anyone you interact with from close family members to virtual strangers.

Question for Reflection: Can you think of any situations in which you have observed or experienced the effects of mirror neurons? (Yawning? Taking on the same body posture or body language of another person? Something else?)

———

———

———

NEURAL WIFI AND EMOTIONAL CONTAGION

Emotional contagion—catching a feeling, a mood, or the impulse to take action--is something we can all recognize in our daily lives. You may have observed it in yourself if you've felt the excitement at your college football game, or if you have participated in singing an emotionally moving song with a group of people, or if you've been in a crowd that is in a panic to escape from a dangerous situation. If it was a pleasant situation, you may have wished that you could keep that "good feeling" for a longer time.

On a more everyday basis, you may feel the contagion of emotion when you sit down at the table with an angry teenager or spouse, or as you observe someone sobbing with grief, or when you see a child's face light up with a smile of delight when she has taken her first solo bike ride. We are affected by others' emotions whether we are aware of it or not!

It is the system of mirror neurons that help explain this familiar sense of sharing emotions with other beings. The neural bridge that is created between brains is like a "neural wifi." Emotions can pass from person to person without anyone consciously noticing. That is why we can sometimes feel emotionally "hijacked." Our brains respond to what we see and hear before we have had enough time to think about what has happened.

Question for Reflection: Have you had experiences in which you "catch" the emotion of others (it could be one person or a crowd of thousands)? Where have you observed the contagion of emotion?

_____

_____

_____

_____

Resource: Connected: *The Surprising Power of Our Social Networks and How They Shape Our Lives*, Nicholas Christakis and James Fowler, 2011, Back Bay Books.

EXPERIENCE EMOTIONAL CONTAGION FOR YOURSELF

You can experience and observe this phenomenon of emotional contagion for yourself by watching a few brief videos.

BABIES LAUGHING

https://www.youtube.com/watch?v=L49VXZwfup8 (3:07 minutes)

The first one, "Best Babies Laughing Video Compilation," gives us the sense that there is a good evolutionary reason for mirror neurons since humans need to understand what others are feeling. This is especially true when we are helpless infants, but the need to read others' feelings does not end there.

GET YOUR EMOTIONAL JUICES FLOWING

https://youtube.com/watch?v=orukqxeWmM0 (4:05 minutes)

See if this video gets your emotional juices flowing! As you watch more than 13,000 people in Trafalgar Square (London) singing the old Beatles' song, "Hey Jude," pay attention to how they are feeling—and then take a moment to ask yourself how you are feeling after watching the video.

CHRISTIAN THE LION

https://www.youtube.com/watch?v=md2CW4qp9e8 (2:36 minutes)

Here is another example of the power of emotion and the fact that emotions are contagious. As you watch the video, be an observer of your emotions!

"Christian the Lion," long a YouTube favorite, is about a lion who was adopted (from a London department store!) as a cub, grew too large to take care of in London, and was shipped to a new home on an African game farm. As you watch the video, look for evidence of emotion as you observe the faces of the two young men who adopted the lion, and be an observer of your own emotions as well.

Question for Reflection: How did you feel as you watched each of the videos? Did you observe and feel the contagion of emotion?

_____

_____

IMPLICATIONS OF EMOTIONAL CONTAGION FOR LEADERSHIP

Remember—we *all* have the potential to serve as leaders in various contexts. Think of what this emotional contagion and the ability to influence how others feel can mean for all those who take on a leadership role:

- In the family
- In schools and colleges
- In business
- In sports
- In politics and government
- In entertainment
- In religion
- In healthcare
- In the military
- In volunteer groups

While leaders may have an edge for affecting how others feel, anyone can have an impact on emotions—and actions—of others.

Question for Reflection: Do leaders have "an edge" in affecting the emotions of others just because they are the designated leaders? Can you think of an example from your own experience?

_____

_____

_____

_____

_____

_____

THE SUCCESS MODEL OF EMOTIONAL INTELLIGENCE

The Success Model of Emotional Intelligence is based on reading, research, and observation. The graphic below indicates the five inter-related aspects of Emotional Intelligence. The following is a brief overview of the five dimensions of the model, which will be covered in more detail in the later chapters of this book

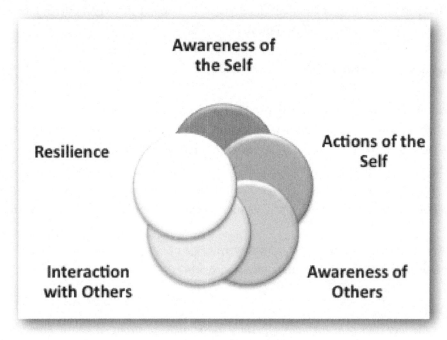

The Success Model has five inter-related dimensions. Probably the biggest difference between the Success Model and most others is that "Resilience," which is often included in other models, plays a stronger role as one of five major aspects of Emotional Intelligence. The good news is that each of the five dimensions can be improved—if you're willing to learn and practice the skills.

It is worth remembering that although building Emotional Intelligence skills can be significant for any individual, an emotionally intelligent workplace needs a whole team of emotionally intelligent individuals to create a truly resonant organization—a workplace that is successful in being productive, creative, and sustainable, and that emphasizes emotional well-being of all employees.

FIVE DIMENSIONS OF THE SUCCESS MODEL
AWARENESS OF THE SELF
Definition: *The ability to identify emotions in yourself and to perceive the impact you have on others.*

Awareness of the Self is basic to the concept of Emotional Intelligence. It shows up in every model of Emotional Intelligence—and all the other aspects depend on the strength of self-awareness.

Questions for Exploring Awareness of the Self:

- Do I know when I am looking at a "gray" situation in black and white?
- Can I Identify physical signs in myself of anger, sadness, frustration, elation, satisfaction—and other emotions?
- Can I recognize facial expressions or body language that indicate how people are reacting to my words or behaviors?
- Do I acknowledge to myself moments of joy, disappointment, sadness, jealousy, content—or any other emotions that may come up?
- Am I able to identify the effect that words, smells, pictures, tastes, textures, and sounds (such as music) have on me in the moment?
- Am I aware of when I am speaking or behaving defensively?
- Can I identify my attitude and intent as I communicate with others?

ACTIONS OF THE SELF
Definition: *The ability to manage your own emotions, especially in the midst of strong "negative" emotions in yourself or in your environment.*

This dimension reflects an ability to manage one's emotions in any environment. It may include the ability to anticipate a situation in order to manage your emotions. It may include taking some action that helps you manage a particularly strong emotion.

Questions for Exploring Actions of the Self:

- Am I able to change my thoughts to change my emotions?
- Am I able to step back and see a difficult situation in perspective?
- When I experience "unpleasant" emotions—such as during a conflict situation, can I retain my ability to reflect on what is happening?
- If I feel anxious in a situation, can I plan and implement steps to reduce my anxiety—including the use of humor?
- Can I use internal self-talk to move from a negative emotional state to a positive one?
- Am I able to use my anger in a given situation to be productive?
- Can I give myself a "time out" for relaxation or reflection when the stress is mounting?
- Have I identified my "hot buttons" and found ways to manage my emotions when those buttons are pushed?

AWARENESS OF OTHERS
Definition: *The ability to accurately perceive and understand the emotional states of others*
We learn how others are feeling in various ways—what they say, how they say it, their body language, their facial expressions. When it comes to being aware of how others are feeling, we're all on a spectrum for this ability.

Questions for Exploring Awareness of Others:

- Do I know which individuals will respond negatively to criticism?
- Am I able to anticipate the mood of an individual or a team?
- Can I read "between the lines" of what an individual is saying in order to understand what he or she is experiencing emotionally?
- Am I aware of the personal "lenses" through which an individual or a team may be viewing a certain situation?
- Am I sensitive to how individuals feel about disclosing personal information?
- When I have negative feedback on an individual's performance, am I able to anticipate his or her reaction?
- Do I take the time to observe facial expressions and body postures to understand what people at a meeting may be experiencing?

INTERACTION WITH OTHERS

Definition: *The ability to utilize awareness of others' emotions to build relationships, teams, and support networks*

The reason for being more aware of others' feelings is to have more successful interactions with them—whether it is your family members, your boss, your friends, your colleagues or clients, and anyone else you interact with in the course of your activities each day.

Questions for Exploring Interaction with Others:

- Am I able to read the mood of an individual or a team and plan my communication accordingly?
- Does my own behavior and speech serve as a model for others?
- Do I take the time to acknowledge other' contributions, ideas, and actions?
- Am I able to influence individuals, teams, and organizations based on values and mission?
- Am I able to be a calming influence when an individual or a team is behaving inappropriately?
- Do I honestly encourage feedback from others regarding my decisions or behaviors—even if it is negative?
- If an individual has performed poorly, do I confront the person privately rather than embarrass him or her at a meeting?

RESILIENCE

Definition: *The ability to maintain equilibrium despite the inevitable changes that occur both internally and externally in an individual's life*

Those with greater resilience—optimism, flexibility, creativity, the ability to bounce back and learn from mistakes—will be more self-motivated and will be better able to encourage others and have a positive influence on those around them.

Questions for Exploring Resilience:

- Am I able to build networks of support that can be helpful in times of disappointment?
- Am I open to new ideas and directions even when I have invested time and energy in a particular direction?
- Do I create and maintain an environment that is conducive to both reflection and productivity?
- Have I identified appropriate outlets for my creativity and energy?
- When I am frustrated, irritated, or angry, can I transform those emotions into appropriate and productive action?
- Have I developed the confidence to view problems as interesting challenges?
- When working toward a goal, am I able to cope with setbacks and keep the "big picture" in mind?
- Do I make a habit of analyzing errors in order to learn from mistakes?

Two

Awareness of the Self

BUILDING ON WHAT YOU'VE LEARNED

In this chapter, you'll learn about Awareness of the Self--what it means, how it plays out in real life, and, most importantly, how you can enhance your skills in this dimension if you choose to.

Remember that five dimensions of the Success Model are all closely interrelated. They connect and overlap with each other in various ways. Although we'll be talking about them separately, keep in mind that the skills of each dimension are related and often build on each other.

You might want to take a minute or two now to look back at how you scored on Awareness of the Self on the assessment you took earlier (in Chapter 1). Or, if you have taken a longer assessment, such as the EQ-i, you may want to look at the indicators for your levels of self-awareness. This aspect of Emotional Intelligence is included in all models and is basic to enhancing your Emotional Intelligence in all of its dimensions.

Question for Reflection: How did you score on Awareness of the Self on the assessment in Chapter 1?

_____

_____

_____

EVERYDAY LIFE SCENARIOS

How do the skills of Awareness of the Self--or the lack of such skills--show up in our everyday lives?

First, a couple of examples that are about people who have some strength in self-awareness:

SCENARIO: After a particularly frustrating day at work, Jonathan is no sooner in the house when he starts fuming about his boss and his colleagues. When he sees the look on his wife's face, he stops, laughs a little, and asks her about her day.

SCENARIO: After her son's Little League baseball game during which her son mostly sat on the bench, Jennifer feels like yelling at the coach. Instead, she takes time to reflect on the situation, and what and why she is feeling at the moment.

The following scenarios show people who need development in the skills of self-awareness:

SCENARIO: Dennis, who is going through a difficult time dealing with two somewhat rebellious teenagers as well as with his elderly mother's failing health, goes into work wondering why he is having difficulty responding to routine emails and telephone calls.

SCENARIO: After putting in 14-hour days for weeks on end as a volunteer for a local election campaign, Michelle is surprised one morning to find herself flat on her back with muscle spasms as she tries to get out of bed.

Question for Reflection: Do you recognize any of these strengths or lack of strength in the people you know? In yourself?

_____

_____

_____

_____

_____

_____

DEFINITION: AWARENESS OF THE SELF

Self-awareness is the foundational building block of Emotional Intelligence. The first step in enhancing or building your overall Emotional Intelligence as well as your empathy and compassion for others is achieving a healthy level of self-awareness—which is the ability to identify emotions in the self and to perceive the impact you have on others at home, in the workplace, within the local community, and beyond that if you happen to have a wider sphere of influence.

More specifically, being self-aware means that you can:

- Identify your own feelings
- Recognize how people perceive you
- Recognize how you respond in a variety of situations
- Identify your intent and attitude as you communicate with others

We'll look at each of these more closely and provide suggestions for improving each of these skills.

Question for Reflection: Looking at this list of skills, are there any that you would like to build or improve?

_____

_____

_____

_____

_____

_____

IDENTIFY YOUR FEELINGS

"The most fundamental aggression to ourselves, the most fundamental harm we can do to ourselves, is to remain ignorant by not having the courage and the respect to look at ourselves honestly and gently."

— PEMA CHÖDRÖN

Let's consider the first of these four skills—taking an honest look to identify your own feelings.

The exercise below, "How Would I Feel?" will give you a bit of practice in identifying how you might feel in a variety of situations. Take some time to complete the exercise, and then come back to compare your answers to what others have said.

To increase this skill, get in the habit of asking yourself, "How do I feel right now?" in any situation that comes up. You might even keep a feelings journal to observe and track your progress.

HOW WOULD I FEEL?

For each of the following situations, fill in the blank with an emotion /feeling word or phrase to describe how you would feel in each situation.

1. Situation: You have just been awarded a prestigious honor in your area of expertise.
   I feel _____.

2. Situation: A day after the final interview for a position you really want, you learn that someone else—in fact, a person you have mentored—was offered the job.
   I feel_____.

3. Situation: You finished 49th out of 150 participants in your age group running a marathon.
   I feel_____.

4. Situation: As you are driving to work on a busy freeway, the driver of another car, who is speaking on a cell phone, begins to move into your lane and very nearly side-swipes you.
   I feel_____.

5. Situation: You are at your desk working on a project when the phone rings; the police have arrested your teenage son/ daughter for drunk driving.
   I feel _____.

6. Situation: You get the results of a 360-degree feedback; all of your raters except for one have given you high ratings in all categories. The one exception is a low rating in the areas of trust and integrity.
   I feel _____.

LET'S COMPARE FEELINGS

What was it like putting yourself into these situations? Certain ones may have been familiar to you, but you probably had to use your imagination and your ability to empathize in others on the list.

How did you do at putting a *name* to your feelings? If you found it easy, good for you. You have an advantage on the road to greater Emotional Intelligence. If identifying your feelings was difficult, don't worry. This is a skill that you can practice and improve.

Let's take a look at a few of the items on the "How Would I Feel?" exercise:

1.   The first situation on the worksheet seems to be a pleasurable one—being awarded an honor in your area of expertise. Did you ever wonder what it would be like to get a phone call—let's say from the White House—in which someone tells you that you have been awarded a national honor? What would you feel if you got such a call?

      If you are among the majority who answered this item, the words you chose are quite positive—delighted, happy, honored, proud. Some people, however, also express surprise or even shock, and a few express humility—usually explained by the fact that they alone don't deserve the credit, but rather it should be shared. All of these different feelings may be honest expressions for those who are feeling them.

2.   In the second situation, someone you have mentored gets the job you were hoping for. This one is a bit more complex. Let's imagine that you've just seen the announcement on email. Mary Smith or John Doe will take over duties as Vice President of Marketing (or whatever position you were hoping for). How do you feel?

      Did you write down more than one feeling for this one? Many respondents report an initial feeling of anger, jealousy, or resentment. But many also report a secondary feeling of pride in the person they have mentored—or even some happiness for them. By the way, note that we will not label these emotions as either "positive" or "negative." All feelings, all emotions, can provide us with useful information. Then it is up to us to reflect and take action based on that information.

3.   In the third situation, you are asked to imagine that you have run a marathon and have finished 49th among 150 entrants in your age group. There are usually three categories of answers to this situation.

      One group—whether they are actually runners or not-- express feelings such as happiness, relief, pride, a sense of accomplishment.

      Another group—usually people who are actually runners with well-worn running shoes to show for it—express some disappointment in only placing 49th in their age group. Even some people who are not runners express disappointment in only placing in 49th place.

      A third group—which includes people like me who do not run for either pleasure or health—express feelings like ecstasy, incredulity, amazement—mostly because we are shocked to imagine ourselves finishing a marathon at all!

Question for Reflection: How easy (or how difficult) was it for you to identify your feelings as you imagined yourself in these six scenarios?

_____

_____

_____

_____

_____

SAME SITUATION, DIFFERENT FEELINGS

The point of all this is a simple one, but it will prove to be a significant one as we explore the concepts of Emotional Intelligence: *Not everyone feels the same in a given situation.*

Can you imagine yourself holding a tarantula—you know, one of those large, furry black spiders? Use your imagination to enter this situation: You are holding this black tarantula in your palm. You feel it walking on the skin of your hand. You feel each leg move as the creature crawls unto your fingers.

Some people may feel quite comfortable holding the spider. Others may feel curious and a bit excited. Others may feel fearful and disgusted. How would *you* feel in this moment?

In a later chapter, we'll talk about being aware of others' emotions by observing facial expressions and body language, but here we are inviting you to simply observe that people can feel quite differently about the same situation.

Not everyone feels the same in a given situation. Same situation, different feelings. You might try out the list of situations on "How Would I Feel?" with family or colleagues. You may be surprised to find how differently people react to the same situation.

How can you increase this skill to honestly identify your feelings? Remember, the reason for identifying your feelings is so that you can learn to manage them.

There are over 4,000 words in the English language to describe feelings, but it takes practice to be honest with yourself and accurately identify how you feel.

Being able to identify and describe feelings and emotions in the moment is a first step in achieving healthy sense of self-awareness. We refer to this as "emotional literacy."

If you want to see a comprehensive list of feeling words, go to this website: http://www.eqi.org/fw.htm

FEELINGS ARE NOT THOUGHTS, LABELS, OR BEHAVIORS

Note: The following are *not* the expression of feelings! (Hint: Don't use "like" or "that" as you express how you feel.)

- I feel like (choking him, hugging her, quitting, screaming) That is behavior, *not* a feeling.
- I feel like (an idiot, a child, a fifth wheel) That is a label, *not* a feeling.
- I feel that (you are unreasonable, this is a waste of time, we've done all this before) That is a thought, *not* a feeling.

So—pause for a moment here and try answering this question for yourself:

How am I feeling right now, in this moment? At this moment I feel _____.

FEELINGS	NOT FEELINGS
Safe	
Helpless	I feel *like* throwing my computer out the window.
Delighted	
Miserable	
Energetic	
Intrigued	I feel *like* a rat in a trap.
Frustrated	
Disgusted	
Surprised	
Frightened	I feel *that* you are being unreasonable.
Pleased	
Satisfied	

There are, of course, an enormous number of possibilities for words to describe how you feel. But it's not always easy to come up with the honest expression of feeling in the moment. See which of these three scenarios best describes you:

1. QUICK TO IDENTIFY FEELINGS

You may be among those who are quickly able to come up with what you feel. You may also be aware of physical sensations that help you interpret how you are feeling—fidgety if you are impatient, wide-awake and attentive if you are curious, and a bit sleepy or distracted by other things in your environment if you are bored—playing a game or sending a text on your smartphone perhaps?

2. REFLECTIVE

Or you may be among those who need more reflection to understand your emotions and you can't come up with a descriptive word or phrase quickly. Perhaps instead of "I feel (some specific emotion such as bored or curious)" you are accustomed to saying things like "I feel like" --I feel like eating a candy bar or I feel like taking a coffee break OR you have a thought such as: I feel like this will be helpful to me—or not helpful as the case may be. If you are in this category, I encourage you to go back to the "I feel [an emotion] model. Try to identify the feeling—the emotion, not a thought, or a label, or a behavior. Instead try: I feel hurt. I feel delighted. I feel jealous.

3. DIFFICULTY IN IDENTIFYING EMOTIONS

There is a third group of people—not as populous as the first two. If you are in this group, you may have difficulty not only express-ing emotions but even identifying them to yourself even when you've taken time to reflect. This is a condition that has roots in both nature and nurture and not a topic we'll be covering in depth here. But because Awareness of the Self—and the ability to identify your own emotions—is basic to healthy Emotional Intelligence, we urge you to explore how this may limit you in managing your own emotions and in navigating your relationships with others. And remember that this is a skill that can be learned, but like any skill, it takes practice.

LEARNING FROM OTHER PEOPLE'S FEELINGS

Did you ever wonder why journalists are always asking people how the feel—whether they have won the lottery or the Super Bowl or an Olympic medal? Or, on the other hand—if they are the survivors of a catastrophe such as a hurricane or a plane crash or a flood? Journalists know that we are curious—intrigued even—by how people feel in extreme situations—whether joyous or tragic. In fact, watching and listening to how other people feel is one of the ways we learn about feelings—both our own and others.

In January of 2009, Captain "Sully" Sullenberger piloted a US Airways passenger jet to a safe landing in the icy cold waters of the Hudson River after the plane collided with birds soon after take-off, disabling the plane's jet engines.

All 155 crew and passengers survived the event. You may have heard some of these interviews of passengers, crew, and of Captain Sullenberger himself.

We all wanted to know the details of what happened—but what did we most want to know?

In an interview on "60 Minutes," journalist and news anchor Katie Couric asked Captain Sullenberger: "Did you think, 'How are we going to get ourselves out of this?" He answered, "No. My initial reaction was one of disbelief."

Now—is "disbelief" an emotion? More likely it is a thought that quickly followed a feeling of shock or panic or fear. Sullenberger went on to try to describe his feelings: "It was the worst sickening pit-of-your-stomach, falling through the floor feeling I've ever felt in my life," . . . I knew immediately it was very bad." Being aware of changes in your physiology—your body—is a good first step in identifying your feelings, your emotions.

It's not always easy to identify what we are feeling in the moment. Notice that Captain Sullenberger made up phrases to describe his extraordinary experience: "sickening pit-of-the-stomach, falling through the floor feeling." Instead of revealing an emotion such as fear or fright, Captain Sullenberger is attempting to tell us how the emotion showed up in his physical self—the pit of his stomach—and the thought that followed that awareness.

THREE THINGS TO LEARN FROM A PLANE CRASH

You may be interested in listening to another survivor of that same flight, a passenger named Ric Elias. By the time he gave this TED talk, he had plenty of time for reflection, of course, but see if you can sort out his feelings from his thoughts.

3 Things I Learned While My Plane Crashed (5:03 minutes)

https://www.youtube.com/watch?v=8_zk2DpgLCs

Question for Reflection: What reactions did you have to this video?

_____

_____

_____

_____

_____

_____

QUICK REVIEW

Ric Elias's account of his experience in a plane about to crash land provides us with that vicarious window into the feelings of another person. As you listened, you may have been asking yourself: How would I feel if I were in an airplane about to make a crash landing? And you may also be asking, as Ric Elias prompts us to do—what effect would such an experience have on my life?

We don't need a disaster or a catastrophe, of course, to become more aware of how we feel. But considering these situations can help us remember a couple of key points.

Just as a review and reminder, try filling in the blanks below. (Answers at bottom of page)

A. Same situation – different _____

We react to events differently—based on our own life experiences, our attitudes, our physiology, our knowledge, as well as the situation itself.

B. A good first step in becoming more aware of my emotions is to try to _____.

C. Learning to be more aware of feelings (and actually *naming* them) is a good first step to being able to _____ them.

Answers: A. feelings (or emotions) B. identify them (or name them) C. manage (or change)

RECOGNIZE HOW OTHERS PERCEIVE YOU

"When it comes to ourselves, we often have a blind spot. That is, we fail to see ourselves as others see us. We fail to recognize our most obvious traits: our strengths, weaknesses, mannerisms."

— MARK LINK, CHALLENGE: A DAILY MEDITATION PROGRAM

A second skill in Awareness of the Self is *recognizing how people perceive you.* You may be wondering—how can I know how others see me? This, too, is a skill that can be learned. It will take some practice in being a keen observer—of others, but also of yourself.

A STORY ABOUT SELF-AWARENESS

Not long ago, after getting off a flight from a relaxing, stress-free vacation in sunny Mexico, I found myself in a slow-moving line at U.S. Customs. With no attempt to eavesdrop, I couldn't help but hear a conversation taking place less than two feet behind me—apparently two businessmen discussing one of their colleagues—or more likely, one of their employees.

"That was just not funny in the least," said the gray-haired and rather distinguished looking man who was clearly feeling outraged. "This isn't the first time, and taking that picture there in the airport was the final straw," he went on. "What was she thinking? It's time to get rid of her."

The other fellow did not have the same sense of outrage, but neither did he seem to want to contradict the man who may have been his boss. After a few minutes of listening and kind of grunting his assent, he tried changing the subject. But then the outraged guy was right back at it. "She's entertaining, and she's smart, but she just doesn't know her limits. That was not funny at all. There have been too many incidents. We're going to have to do something."

It was all I could do not to swing my head around and get a closer look at these two guys. And I would have loved to know what it is that the smart, funny woman (I was picturing an attractive woman—perhaps Generation X or Y) had said or done to make this man angry enough to blast his feelings to any number of people dragging their suitcases through Customs.

In his anger—it was clear that the woman under discussion had somehow touched a hot button—he wasn't aware or didn't care who heard him as he planned his revenge out loud. At that moment, I was wishing that I could call the woman, whoever she was, and warn her that her behavior had been perceived as threatening and that if she wanted to keep her job, she had better modify her words, actions, and attitude around her boss.

Then it occurred to me that both the man (whom I assume to be the boss) and the woman (whom I assume to be an employee) are suffering from the same problem—a *lack of self-awareness.* Self-awareness is the foundational piece of Emotional Intelligence. A lack of it can cause problems in other areas—managing one's emotions, understanding what others are feeling, building satisfying relationships with others, and even having the resilience that is needed to cope with the inevitable changes and challenges that are part of life. Self-awareness matters, a lot.

I don't know the true and doubtless complicated story of the man in the Customs line, but in the story I created about him after listening to his tirade for ten minutes or more, I think I can say that he is not self-aware. He probably cannot find the words to describe how he is feeling in the moment. He may have been surprised to learn that the employee—the woman who behaved so boldly—perceives him in a way that does not match his perception of himself. He did not seem aware that the man listening to him on line was uncomfortable—not to mention those of us strangers who were standing in close proximity.

Such lack of self-awareness makes this distinguished gentleman appear much like a two-year old who has been thwarted in some way. I imagine that he is an intelligent man, a business executive, perhaps the owner of his own business. He may work very hard and even have taken his employees to a retreat at a resort in a sunny clime. But I also imagine that he finds himself confused by an inability to relate to the people around him. He may have similar difficulties relating to his family members. I imagine that instead of trying to understand those with whom he lives and works, he falls back on his authority—as a father, as a boss—but that he is left feeling dissatisfied and even isolated.

And what about the woman who may have been fired on Monday? I don't know her real story either, but the story I've created about her tells me that she, too, lacks self-awareness. And that lack is going to get her into trouble sooner or later. She is smart, she is entertaining—so says the man who does not find her funny. She may not be aware, however, of her own intentions and attitudes as she jokes or kids her colleagues. She may also not be aware of how others perceive her, even as they are laughing. She may feel that being smart—perhaps she is a graduate of Yale or Stanford or Duke—is enough, and that she doesn't have to care about others' emotions.

These stories are fictions imagined from brief observations, but they might be true. Haven't we all observed and known people who lack this self-awareness? The good news is that self-awareness isn't a genetically transmitted character trait. Self-awareness can be taught, and it can be learned. From early childhood forward, we have been learning to be more self-aware, and many of us still have a few lessons to learn. Self-awareness matters, a lot.

Being aware of how you are being perceived by others is a significant aspect of Awareness of the Self. And I don't mean only for politicians and leaders and other people who are have the opportunity to speak in public. An accurate appraisal of how others perceive you is also important to building relationships, teams, and support networks in everyday life—and in the workplace.

Question for Reflection: Do you have a trusted friend or colleague help you discover your "blind spots"?

_____

_____

_____

_____

_____

RECOGNIZE YOUR TYPICAL RESPONSES

Another skill that can help you increase your Emotional Intelligence in the dimension of Awareness of the Self is enhancing your understanding of how you respond to people in a variety of situations.

REACTING TO A COMPLAINER

For example, let's say you have a co-worker who constantly complains—about everything from the burnt coffee in the break room to the new memo from the boss about a team building retreat. Let's imagine that today this person greets you with an angry complaint: "Now they're expecting us to use this new electronic tracking system. It's a waste of time, and I am just going to refuse to do it!" How do you respond? Does this push a hot button for you?

Perhaps the person in this particular scenario wouldn't bother you much. Perhaps you would offer some assistance to the complainer—or ignore him—or simply laugh it off. But you may also have found it quite annoying or upsetting.

REACTING TO AN ANGRY DRIVER

I know a fellow who seems hyper-alert to the errors of other drivers—for example, someone who fails to put on a turn signal when changing lanes, or someone who rushes through a yellow light at the last moment. This fellow becomes angry with the drivers, calls them nasty names, and sometimes honks the car horn. He cannot *not* react this way. It is his typical response.

WHAT CAN THIS DO FOR ME?

Becoming more aware of your typical response to a variety of situations will help build your self-awareness. Even if you don't find any of these situations particularly relevant, perhaps you will be able to think of some people and/or situations that seem to call forth a usual response from you—annoyance, anger, or perhaps even rage.

If you become more aware of how you typically respond, you can choose to modify that response to build better relationships and to gain better outcomes—with family, friends, business colleagues, customers, and anyone with whom you interact.

Try the following exercise, "My Typical Responses," and take a few minutes to think about how you usually respond in the given situations.

MY TYPICAL RESPONSES
Here's another angle on self-observation—which can lead to greater self-awareness.

ASK YOURSELF: HOW PREDICTABLE AM I?
You could learn a lot about yourself by asking this question of someone who knows you well—a spouse or partner, a trusted colleague, your teenager, your golf buddy, or your bridge partner. But you can learn even more by asking this question of yourself and becoming a keen *observer of your own emotions.*

Try this exercise, and in the weeks ahead, come back to your answers to match your "typical responses" to real life situations you may have encountered. For each of these eight situations, write what you would typically feel, and then answer the related questions.

1. You open your mail and learn that you made an error on your income tax form; you will be getting a large refund.

- Feeling/Emotion _____
- Is this feeling helpful to you? _____
- Does this feeling have any negative consequences for you? _____

2. Your boss tells you that you may be laid off at the end of the month.

- Feeling/Emotion _____
- Is this feeling helpful to you? _____
- Does this feeling have any negative consequences for you? _____

3. You view a particularly beautiful sunset or sunrise.

- Feeling/Emotion _____
- Is this feeling helpful to you? _____
- Does this feeling have any negative consequences for you? _____

4. An airline employee informs you that your flight home after a week-long conference has been canceled.

- Feeling/Emotion _____
- Is this feeling helpful to you? _____
- Does this feeling have any negative consequences for you? _____

5. The person ahead of you in the grocery store line sees that you have only a couple items and graciously says, "Please, go ahead of me."

- Feeling/Emotion _____
- Is this feeling helpful to you? _____
- Does this feeling have any negative consequences for you? _____

6. Tomorrow you will give a report on your department's work to the organization's executive team.

- Feeling/Emotion _____
- Is this feeling helpful to you? _____
- Does this feeling have any negative consequences for you? _____

7. You are in a fast-food restaurant when you see an elderly person slip and fall. You rush to the person's side, call for emergency help, and stay to comfort the person until help arrives.

- Feeling/Emotion _____
- Is this feeling helpful to you? _____
- Does this feeling have any negative consequences for you? _____

8. Traffic slows to a crawl on the freeway, and you know you'll be at least an hour late for a dinner appointment.

- Feeling/Emotion _____
- Is this feeling helpful to you? _____
- Does this feeling have any negative consequences for you? _____

IDENTIFY INTENT AND ATTITUDE IN YOUR COMMUNICATION

Children can be pretty honest about showing their feelings—frowns, whines, even tantrums. If they don't like something or feel hurt or angry, they don't usually hide those feelings. As adults, we learn to be more subtle about our feelings, often believing that we are hiding what we actually feel. Sometimes, however, we may not be clear about our own intent and attitude as we communicate, nor are we aware of the message that we are conveying to others.

There is one more skill that plays a part in Awareness of the Self. It is the ability to identify your intent and attitude as you communicate with others. What exactly does this mean? Let's look at some of the ways people communicate what seems to be "information" but has some obvious "attitude" or other intent that is communicated along with the information.

We all do this sort of thing, and there is no need to "judge" these behaviors—but it may be useful to be aware that we often communicate much more than the words we are speaking. Here are some examples:

- **Name dropping**

We name drop—people we know, the prestigious educational institution we went to, the name of the sorority or fraternity we belonged to—or even the celebrities we've met or at least sighted! To grow in self-awareness, ask: What is my intent as I provide this information?

- **Impressing others with knowledge, money, social status, possessions, and children's or grandchildren's accomplishments**

Again, we all do this to some extent—and for the most part, in our western society it is allowable—up to a certain limit. We all know people who go overboard and seem too intent on displaying their superior status. Do you have friends who post a few too many of their accomplishments on social media? How do you feel about those long holiday letters?

- **Making others feel sorry for you—perhaps even making yourself appear helpless**

A rather different group of people like to tell us their woes—their surgical operations, their disappointments in relationships, their money troubles, their mistreatment by a teacher or a boss. We all share these life events with some family or friends, but some people don't seem to censor what they say or to whom. And they seem to like appearing helpless, perhaps so that others will rescue them.

- **Garnering attention for yourself when someone else is getting attention**

Have you ever started telling someone about your vacation or something clever your child or grandchild did only to be cut off by that person who would rather speak about her own trip or his own children rather than listen to you? We often refer to this as one-upmanship—a kind of "I can match that and go one better!" What is the intent behind the words in that situation?

- **Making the other person feel a certain way—stupid, unnecessary, a fool, behind the times, out of the loop, unattractive**

We all knew someone like this in junior high school—often it was a bully. And even then we probably recognized that the person put others down to make himself or herself feel bigger and better in some way. The people who are still doing this as adults, however--and they are doing it in offices, in hospitals, in universities, in any place you can think of--people with this behavior can improve their self-awareness to learn more effective ways of gaining self-esteem while also finding more satisfaction in relating to others. In that way, increased self-awareness improves the environment for everyone involved.

All of this adds up to the idea that knowing the intent and attitude behind what you say to others is an important part of Awareness of the Self—and just one of the ways you can enhance your level of Emotional Intelligence in this dimension.

Question for Reflection: Do you recognize any of these attitudes in your own behavior or in the behavior of others?

_____

_____

_____

_____

_____

TRY JUST ONE!

Below are several suggestions for improving your self-awareness. Don't try them all at once. Instead, choose one or two that appeal to you. Be sure to keep track of the results of any action you decide to take.

1. Take a few minutes to list the feelings you had in a single day--or a week, if you have time for that!

The ability to identify how you are feeling is the first step in managing (not "controlling") your emotions. It's not always easy to identify what you are feeling, especially if you experience more than one emotion--anger and love for a wayward teenager for example,. By writing down your feelings, you may see a pattern emerge, and that recognition will help you grow in self-awareness.

2. At your next meeting (with an individual or with a group), observe the impact that your words, facial expressions, tone of voice, and body language have on others.

Try out your powers of observation! Take close notice of how the other person's facial expression and body language change as you are speaking. Then, at another meeting, try doing one thing differently--perhaps speaking in a softer tone, for example. Or looking more directly at the person as you speak. Can you notice any change?

3. Ask a trusted colleague to be a "shadow coach" to observe you and then give you constructive feedback about your inter-actions, your facial expressions, and your body language.

Being aware of how you feel and how others perceive you is a foundational aspect of Emotional Intelligence. Hiring a coach or just asking someone you trust to observe you in meetings, for example, can provide you with new information about how your words, expressions, behaviors, and decisions affect the people you work with every day.

4. Participate in a 360-degree feedback survey with your colleagues, boss, and direct reports to compare how you perceive your behavior and actions with how others perceive those same behaviors and actions.

It takes courage to participate in a 360-degree feedback survey, but you will learn a great deal about how others see you--and increase your awareness of self. Do others feel that you have what it takes to be a leader? Are you an empathetic listener? Do you seem indecisive to those around you? Can people trust you to do what you say you will do?

5. Before a presentation, video yourself as you practice speaking before a group.

What do your facial expressions, your body language, and your voice say about you when you speak at a meeting, during a discussion, or presenting at a conference? Be your own helpful observer and critic as you watch a video of your rehearsal. You will learn some interesting things about yourself and how you come across to others.

6. After a difficult encounter with someone, take time to analyze what you are feeling.

Being aware of what you are feeling as you are feeling it is the first step to being able to manage that feeling. Pay attention to what your body is telling you (upset stomach? headache? hands shaking?) as you try to name the feeling. There are over 3000 words in the English language to describe feelings--but we use so few of them!

7. Take time to list your values (adventure, connection, peace, financial security?)--whatever matters most to you--for the next "chapter" of your life.

Taking the time to list your values for "the next chapter" (that can be six months, six years, however you define it) can help you gain clarity around what is really important to you. Any decision you make, whether concerning relationships, business, or what to do in your free time is more likely to be informed by these values if you've taken the time to think about them and write them down.

8. Take a survey of your strengths and plan to consciously use them more on a daily basis.

There are any number of surveys that you can buy or find on the Internet for free. Try taking the VIA Survey of Character Strengths at:

www.authentichappiness.sas.upenn.edu

Knowing and using your strengths can be just as important as improving upon those areas where you could improve.

WHAT DID YOU LEARN?

Let's take a minute to summarize and reflect on the main ideas about the foundational dimension, Awareness of the Self.

1. **Same situation – Different feelings**

   The very fact that not all of us react in the same way to the same situation—a political speech, a beautiful sunset, a rigorous physical workout—helps us understand that our reactions to events can be modified –not only to help us maintain balance and equanimity—but to gain greater success as individuals, as team members, and as members of a larger organization. We can in fact learn this skill—something we'll be talking more about in the next step: Actions of the Self.

2. The **ability to identify emotions/feelings**—to name them--can help you build self-awareness, the foundational building block for enhancing Emotional Intelligence.

3. We talked about four aspects of Awareness of the Self and how you can practice skills to **enhance your self-awareness**:

- **Increase your "emotional literacy."** Try keeping a journal where you jot down a word or two to describe your feelings and emotions in the format "I feel *an emotion.* " Not a label, or a thought, or a behavior.
- **Observe how others perceive you.** It may be easiest to begin your observation with just one person or a small team.
- **Observe how you respond in a variety of situations.** What do you do when someone in your environment is angry? Or when someone tells you some good news of theirs? Or when someone expresses sadness? Or when someone says something sarcastic to you? What about when someone tells a racist or ethnic joke? Practice observing what comes up for you in these and other situations.
- **Observe your intent and attitude as you communicate.** Enhancing this skill takes practice over time, but with some focused self-observation, you can definitely improve.

REFLECTION: AWARENESS OF THE SELF

"We live most of our lives by habit. These habits keep us stuck in patterns that limit our experience of life. Once we detect a pattern we were previously unconscious of, we can choose differently, if we want. With awareness comes choice and with choice, we gain freedom."

--WWW.HIGHERAWARENESS.COM

AWARENESS OF THE SELF:

Self-awareness is the foundational building block of Emotional Intelligence. The first step in enhancing or building your overall Emotional Intelligence is achieving a healthy level of self-awareness—which is the ability to identify emotions in the self and to perceive the impact you have on others at home, in the workplace, within the local community, and beyond that if you happen to have a wider sphere of influence.

More specifically, being self-aware means that you can:

- Identify your own feelings
- Recognize how people perceive you
- Recognize how you respond to people in a variety of situations
- Identify your intent and attitude as you communicate with others

BECOME A KEEN OBSERVER

Increasing your ability to *observe*—both yourself and others—will enhance your Emotional Intelligence. You can practice these skills in your own reflections, in your everyday interactions with others, or even when you watch TV or a movie.

For increased self-awareness, get in the habit of asking yourself:

- What am I feeling as I (interact, listen, speak, make a presentation, etc.)?
- What would this person (or these people) say or feel about me when I've left the room?
- What is my intent as I (interact, listen, speak, make a presentation, etc.)?
- What am I revealing about how I feel in my facial expressions, my body language, and my style of dress?
- What can I do to better make the impact that I intend, and to convey my message?

MAKE A PLAN TO IMPROVE

Reflect on the suggestions below that may be helpful in enhancing your skills in Awareness of the Self. In the final chapter of this book, you will have an opportunity to choose activities for an action plan. At this point, all you need to do is think about whether any of these suggestions could be helpful to you in enhancing your self-awareness.

1. Take time to list your values (what matters most to you) for the next "chapter" of your life.
2. After a difficult personal encounter (boss, spouse, child, friend, stranger), analyze what you are feeling.
3. Hire a "shadow coach" to give you feedback on your time management, your productivity, or your interactions with colleagues.
4. Be aware of when you are thinking negative thoughts. Keep track.

5. Survey your strengths and plan to consciously use them more on a daily basis.

6. Ask a trusted colleague to observe you in meetings and give you honest feedback about your interactions, your facial expressions, your body language, and your influence on the group.

7. In decision-making sessions with your co-workers, make it a habit to ask, "What might be the unintended consequence(s) of this action?"

8. Take a 360-degree feedback survey with your colleagues, boss, and direct reports.

9. Keep track of situations that make you angry or upset, situations that make you feel pleased and happy, and identify the emotions you are feeling.

10. Observe the impact that your words and behaviors—both "positive" and "negative"--have on others. (Begin with one person or a small team.)

11. Take an assessment of your Emotional Intelligence, and follow up by working with a coach to improve your skills.

Three

Actions of the Self

BUILDING ON WHAT YOU'VE LEARNED

If you've come this far and are practicing ways to increase your self-awareness, you've already traveled a long way on the path to greater Emotional Intelligence.

In this chapter, you'll learn about the second part of the model, Actions of the Self, a dimension that directly builds on the foundational skills of self-awareness. In this chapter, you'll learn:

- When it might be worthwhile to consider managing your emotions
- Why emotions are so powerful in our lives
- What factors influence our emotions
- Ways to manage, modify, or even change your typical way of reacting to situations
- Ways to manage an "amygdale hijack"

You might want to take a minute or two now to look back at how you scored on Actions of the Self on the assessment you took earlier in the course.

Question for Reflection: How did you score on Actions of the Self on the assessment in Chapter 1?

DEFINITION: ACTIONS OF THE SELF

Individuals who are strong in this dimension:

- Are able to manage their own emotions
- Can express a range of feelings appropriately
- Are able to plan how to manage strong emotions in a given situation
- Have developed ways to cope with those emotions that are perceived to be "negative" and thus maintain their equilibrium

People are sometimes surprised to learn that they can successfully manage (not "control") even quite dramatic emotions such as anger, jealousy, and sadness.

Being aware of your emotions—in the moment you are feeling them--is a great first step in learning to manage them. If you can identify what it is you are feeling, you can learn to acknowledge the emotion, understand how it may be expressed in your physiology, gain an understanding of why you feel that way, and plan a way to manage it if it involves negative consequences.

EVERYDAY LIFE SCENARIOS

How do the skills of Actions of the Self--or the lack of skills--show up in our lives?

The first two scenarios depict people for whom this dimension is a strength:

SCENARIO: After an upsetting argument with her teenager, Miriam drives to work thinking about how to shift her focus from the dramatic emotional argument at home to a major decision that she and her team will be considering today.

SCENARIO: Anticipating challenges that may come up when he talks to his son's teacher, Alberto prepares himself to listen carefully, to keep calm, and to speak honestly but without getting upset. He even rehearses how he might speak to the teacher in front of the mirror as he shaves in the morning.

The next two scenarios depict people who could use some development in this dimension:

SCENARIO: When a neighbor is thoughtlessly critical of Jeanine's new living room furniture, Jeanine gets really quiet and doesn't say anything to her neighbor to defend her taste in home decoration. Later that evening she is furious and even close to tears as she complains to her husband about the neighbor's criticism.

SCENARIO: When an employee speaks up in strong disagreement with a solution that Michael has presented, Michael feels the blood rushing to his face, and when he responds, he has difficulty controlling the sarcastic tone and loud volume of his voice.

Question for Reflection: Do you recognize any of these strengths or lack of strength in the people you know?

_____

_____

_____

_____

_____

_____

WHAT EMOTIONS NEED MANAGING?

"When I say manage emotions, I only mean the really distressing, incapacitating emotions. Feeling emotions is what makes life rich. You need your passions."

—DANIEL GOLEMAN

All emotions provide us with information, and it is worthwhile paying attention to that information. Even the emotions that are sometimes labeled "negative" can lead to positive consequences. Consider the emotion of anger, for example. We have far too many examples in the media of the negative consequences of anger, which we mostly associate with violence, whether in the news, on TV programs, or in movies.

But anger has a positive side as well. Studies in psychology have found that anger can help people deal with relationship problems, can provide momentum in business deals, and can serve as the basis for positive action political agendas. Expressing anger in an appropriate way may even give people a sense of control in an uncertain environment. Historically, anger has motivated cultural change, including the struggle for civil rights and for women's suffrage in the United States.

"Imagine what the women's suffrage movement would have been like if women had said, 'Guys, it's really so unfair, we're nice people and we're human beings too. Won't you listen to us and give us the vote?"

--CAROL TAVRIS, PHD, AUTHOR OF *ANGER: THE MISUNDERSTOOD EMOTION*

Take a moment now to ask yourself this question: Are you able to manage your emotions effectively? Have you had moments when you wish you could have managed better? Note that I say "manage" and not "control." We can't "control" them in the sense of banishing them or ignoring them—but we can make them work for us—first by being aware of them, and then by developing new behaviors including changing our thoughts or our self-talk to manage them.

Question for Reflection: Are you able to manage your emotions effectively? Have you had moments when you wish you could have managed better?

_____

_____

EMOTIONS. ARE. POWERFUL.

Before we begin thinking about where emotions come from and what we can do to manage them, let's acknowledge that emotions are powerful and they are everywhere—in the home, in the workplace, in the political sphere, in our own minds, and in all our interactions with others.

In your imagination, try placing yourself in this situation:

> You are at the airport waiting for your flight. Your attention is drawn to a group of people who are gathered around a soldier. You move closer to observe them. At the center of the group, you see the soldier, dressed in camouflage and boots, hugging a tiny baby. The soldier is kneeling on the floor and crying.

What emotions do you feel? Depending on your own unique life experiences, abilities, genetic makeup, and knowledge, you may feel excited, unsafe, miserable, ecstatic, adventurous, frightened, exhausted, or sad—or some other feeling. Just reading about the soldier and baby, and projecting yourself into the situation can give you a glimpse of just how powerful emotions are.

Question for Reflection: What emotion(s) do you feel imagining yourself in this situation? Be as specific as you can as you *name* the emotions you feel.

_____

_____

_____

_____

_____

_____

EMOTIONS MAKE THE DIFFERENCE

The film, *Historia de un Letrero* (Story of a Sign), was entered in a contest as a film short-short at the Cannes Film Festival. It is a beautiful illustration of the power of emotion.

"Historia de un letero" (The story of a sign) (5:56 minutes)

https://www.youtube.com/watch?v=hMas8TjqeUQ

I hope you will take the time to go watch this short film. Then answer the following question.

Question for Reflection: What is it that made people want to put money in the blind man's cup after the young man rewrote the sign?

_____

_____

_____

_____

_____

_____

WHERE DO THOSE EMOTIONS COME FROM?

We're well aware that people react differently even in the exact same situation. We can observe examples of this every day—at an office meeting, in the supermarket, at the gym, on the ski slopes—anywhere that people react to something in the environment.

Not long ago, we watched a man (somewhere in middle-age) on the ferry who got up to scold a group of ten-year old boys for tossing a soccer ball around in the galley. The chaperones tried calmly to excuse the boys, but the fellow doing the scolding became quite angry. When other passengers spoke up in defense of the boys ("I was sitting right next to them—they didn't bother me!"), the man got angrier still. He finally walked away, still fuming and looking for someone to agree with his point of view. We can only wonder in such a situation about what it is that has made this one person react so strongly when no one else felt the same way.

As another example, consider people's reactions to a natural disaster such as an earthquake, a hurricane, a tornado, or a flood. If you haven't experienced any of these yourself, chances are that you've seen them on TV or read about them in the news. People involved in these extreme situations probably experience a range of emotions over time. Some of the possible reactions include:

- A sense of unreality, perhaps everything seeming surreal
- Fear
- Panic
- Anger
- Loss of control
- Despair
- Anxiety
- Uncertainty
- Disorientation
- Generosity toward others who are suffering in the situation
- Cooperation and camaraderie with those working to relieve the problems
- Exhaustion
- Grief
- Depression
- Guilt (for having survived when others died)
- Gratitude (for having survived)

But what do we know about the reasons for these different reactions? Why do some people feel certain emotions on the list—say panic and despair, while others may be quite frightened but are able to feel generosity and cooperation? When it's all over, why do some people sink into depression, while others are able to begin rebuilding and looking forward with optimism?

Let's consider what factors influence all these emotions, which are intertwined in all our daily activities and interactions.

FACTORS THAT INFLUENCE OUR EMOTIONS

Our emotions are influenced by both internal and external factors. Many of these factors are outside of our consciousness and out of our control. Nevertheless, it is helpful to look into their origins to understand why we feel the way we do.

Internal factors include mental, spiritual, and physical aspects of the self. What you think and know, what you believe and value, and what you experience in your body all have great influence on how you feel—when you hold a baby in your arms, when you sit astride a motorcycle, when you listen to a dramatic piece of music, when you read a murder mystery. We bring ourselves to each of these experiences, so each person's reaction may differ from another's.

Research in psychology, neuroscience, and medicine adds to our understanding of these differences. Here are just a few examples of internal factors that have been studied within the past century or so and remain promising pathways to further understanding our emotions:

- Self-image
- Hormonal fluctuations
- Brain neurotransmitters
- Brain dominance
- Damage to the brain
- Genetic factors (temperament, personality)
- Dietary factors (deficiency or imbalance in vitamins and minerals)
- Sleep deprivation

Question for Reflection: What other internal factors can you think of that affect your emotions?

_____

_____

_____

EXTERNAL FACTORS INFLUENCE EMOTIONS TOO

External factors that influence our emotions include many aspects of society and culture. These factors can have both a positive and a negative impact. We can manipulate them to a limited degree, but it is difficult to eliminate all the negatives. There are some factors that we openly complain about and seek to change or improve. Often, however, we are complacent and unaware of the sometimes negative impact that these factors have on our emotions and behavior:

- Education (and the lack of education)
- Imbalances rooted in role or class differences—especially poverty
- Relationships—family, friends, workplace colleagues, communities
- Technology (and stimulus overload)
- Medication
- Illness
- Diet
- Physical security (crime, danger, violence)
- Financial security (and the lack of security)
- Weather and climate

Question for Reflection: Can you think of other external factors that affect how you feel?

_____

_____

_____

_____

IN PURSUIT OF HAPPINESS

The recent outpouring of books and articles on the topic of happiness—how to get it, how to keep it, what it means, who has it, whether it is possible, and so on—is a good indication of how intent we humans are on managing our emotions.

Take a look at the following list and think about what factors you are conscious of using to manage how you feel. (You may not define your goal as "happiness," but you may want to feel "satisfied," "fulfilled," "content," "safe" or "peaceful.")

At this point, we don't need to judge any of these activities—but simply understand how we are all engaged in regulating and manipulating how we feel:

- Laughter and humor
- Exercise
- Education
- Reading
- Relationships
- Sexual activity
- Work (and gaining financial security)
- Safety
- Food
- Enjoying the natural world
- Gambling
- Music or drama
- Meditation or prayer
- Drugs (legal and illegal)
- Alcohol
- Buying things (from gadgets and clothes to cars, boats, and houses)
- Joyous occasions and celebrations
- Massage and relaxation techniques
- Psychotherapy

Question for Reflection: What factors are you conscious of using in order to modify or manage your feelings?

_____

_____

_____

MANAGING, MODIFYING, AND CHANGING HOW WE FEEL

It is this universal need of humans to feel a certain way (Happiness? Equanimity? Safety?) that brings us to the concepts of Emotional Intelligence. With all our differences and the infinite variety of factors from both nature and nurture, we have the opportunity to observe our emotions and to modify them.

It is not within our purpose here to delve into either the way people respond to extreme circumstances (famine or war, for example) or to study the pathologies of human behavior (clinical depression or obsessive compulsive disorder, for example). Rather, we will take a look at those common emotions of everyday life in both the intrapersonal (your own internal thoughts and emotions) and interpersonal (your interactions with others) realms.

We'll talk about some "hot button" triggers and issues in a few minutes, but let's consider first some general guidelines for managing feelings. There is no one method for handling feelings. If the feeling you have is a pleasant one (joy, gratitude, inspiration, love, generosity), you probably don't need to do anything but enjoy it! This list of suggested steps is for those times when something comes up and you do not have a pleasant feeling:

1. Identify the feeling to bring it to your awareness.
2. Acknowledge the feeling even if you don't like it or aren't proud of it. Write it down or talk to someone about it if appropriate.
3. It the feeling is intense, you may want to take some immediate action: breathe deeply, go for a walk or do some exercise, play music that is soothing to you, drink water, write, look for humor, change the way you talk to yourself, count backwards from fifty, go outside.
4. When you are calmer and can take some time for reflection, ask yourself: What is the price I pay for feeling this way? What can I do to feel differently?

It is important to remember that there may be times when it is not possible to manage your feelings—or at least not manage them well. But you can take the time to learn from those occasions so that you can plan to do something differently the next time a similar situation arises.

Managing emotions is not magic, nor is it a quick fix. It is a process that we all need to attend to throughout our lifetimes. Emotions are neither more nor less intense in our eighties than when we were eight or eighteen. But surely they make our journey interesting.

AMYGDALE HIJACK AND HOT BUTTONS

Sometimes, no matter how emotionally intelligent you are, you may experience an "amygdale hijack." To get an understanding of this term, see if you can imagine yourself as part of this scenario:

> You are a senior executive in your organization. You are in a meeting with your executive team about to make a significant decision to head off a catastrophe. Suddenly, you become aware that two people are texting on their cell phones. You begin to feel anger—and then rage! You can feel the blood rising to your face. You halt discussion and address the texters: "What the (any expletive will do here) do you think you are doing? Get out! Get out now! And don't come back!"

That is an example of the *amygdale hijack*.

A small structure within our brains, the amygdale (actually two structures since we have one in each hemisphere of the brain) is a neural center for emotion. The amygdale is not the only structure involved in emotion, but it can take over the rest of the brain in a millisecond if we feel threatened. Daniel Goleman described the "amygdale hijack" in his 1995 book on Emotional Intelligence.

The amygdale hijack exhibits these three signs:

- Strong emotional reaction
- Sudden onset
- Post-episode realization that the reaction was inappropriate

Question for Reflection: Do you recognize the amygdale hijack? Have you experienced this phenomenon? Have you observed it in someone else?

_____

_____

_____

_____

_____

_____

HOT BUTTONS - AMYGDALE TRIGGERS

"Hot buttons" are part of every person's emotional make-up. They are the triggers for an amygdale hijack. When they are switched "on," your body goes into fight or flight, you shut down, and you want to withdraw or attack. It feels like you are cornered, you focus on one small aspect of what is happening, and you are likely to say things that are less than helpful, or you may simply clam up, afraid to hear what could come out of your mouth.

WHAT ARE YOUR HOT BUTTONS?

What situations or people push your hot buttons—those emotional triggers that can push you to react in unproductive ways? Your "hot buttons" can be pushed by your boss, your colleagues, your employees, and by customers or clients, your spouse, your children, your friends—even a complete stranger.

Sometimes you know immediately that one of your hot buttons has been pushed, but sometimes you may know that you feel bad but are not quite sure why. By identifying your hot button situations and anticipating how you will feel in a particular interaction, you can prepare yourself and manage your reactions.

Do any of the following leave you feeling angry or upset?

A person who . . .

- Is overly dramatic
- Is often sarcastic
- Complains a lot
- Takes all the credit
- Keeps things to himself
- Uses or steps on other people to get ahead
- Is not trustworthy
- Does not ask for information or opinions
- Puts on an act with the boss
- Is blunt and even brutal in speaking his or her opinions
- Often explodes in anger
- Is inconsistent—nice one day, explosive or angry the next
- Preaches about a particular religion, political stance, or philosophy
- Always arrives late to meetings
- Almost never meets deadlines

Question for Reflection: What other hot buttons can you identify?

_____

_____

_____

_____

_____

TOP FIVE AMYGDALE TRIGGERS IN THE WORKPLACE

Did you identify any of these, which Goleman says are the top five amygdale triggers in the workplace?

- Condescension and lack of respect
- Being treated unfairly
- Being unappreciated
- Feeling that you're not being listened to or heard
- Being held to unrealistic deadlines

Question for Reflection: Are any of these present in your life—at home, in the workplace, in the community?

_____

_____

_____

_____

_____

DON'T GET HIJACKED!

You can learn to manage these hot button situations so that you don't feel hijacked by your own emotions. Here are some ideas:

- Realize what's going on (the sooner the better)
- Disengage from the situation
- Monitor what's going on in your own mind and brain and take notice of your reactions
- Notice familiar physical feelings (butterflies in your stomach, blood rushing to your face, headache, etc.)
- Talk yourself out of the hijack—reason with yourself and challenge the "story" that you are telling yourself
- Apply empathy—imagine yourself in that person's position
- Take time for meditation or relaxation exercises
- Replace anger with curiosity
- Observe your reactions as if you were outside yourself

Question for Reflection: What works best for you when you are in danger of an amygdale hijack?

_____

_____

_____

_____

_____

APPLY CURIOSITY

All of us make up stories to explain why something has happened or why another person behaves in a certain way. Sometimes our stories are accurate. Often, they are not! Those stories are what can lead to our hot buttons being pushed. We tell ourselves a story and instantly decide that someone is evil or selfish or ignorant or incompetent—and we react to our own stories.

In the following exercise, "Dealing with Hot Buttons," you have an opportunity to practice one technique for managing hot buttons: replacing anger with curiosity, and becoming more aware of the stories we tell ourselves.

For each scenario:

- Read the scenario and imagine yourself in the situation
- Identify how you feel—and what hot button may have been pushed
- Identify how you feel about the person who pushed your button (what is the story you tell yourself about this person?)
- Use curiosity, empathy and imagination to create another story—which may help to explain that person's behavior

By eliminating the effects of the hot button--your fight or flight response--you will be able to think more clearly to resolve the situation. I am not suggesting that you simply make up nice stories to excuse bad behavior. Rather, use your curiosity to better understand what is causing that other person to behave badly--and then use your logic and cognitive abilities to calmly take action to resolve the issue.

Question for Reflection: Did you find this technique helpful in disarming an amygdale hijack?

_____

_____

_____

_____

_____

DEALING WITH HOT BUTTONS

For each scenario:

- Read the scenario and imagine yourself in the situation
- Identify how you feel—and what hot button may have been pushed
- Identify how you feel about the person who pushed your button (what is the story you tell yourself about this person?)
- Use curiosity, empathy and imagination to create another story—which may help to explain that person's behavior

SCENARIO A:

You work as support staff in the copying and document production shop at a large law firm. You are constantly dealing with associates and partners and very tight deadlines. A few of the firm's attorneys consistently act as if their projects are the only ones you have to take care of, and they behave almost as if you are a machine yourself! One day, one of these impatient attorneys flies off the handle and yells at you when a very last minute copying job has been done incorrectly.

What hot button can you identify?

_____

How do you feel about the attorney who yelled at you?

_____

What explanations can you think of to explain the attorney's behavior?

_____

SCENARIO B:

You are a client services manager for a national mobile phone distributor. You have been working with your team to develop and implement improved customer service strategies. Largely as a result of your team's work, your branch is rated highest in a customer survey administered to all branches of the company. When you attend a meeting of all branch managers and firm executives, you are surprised to hear the Vice President at your branch take all the credit for this outstanding customer service.

What hot buttons can you identify?

_____

How do you feel about the vice president who took all the credit?

_____

What explanation can you think of to explain the vice president's behavior?

_____

SCENARIO C:

You are the director of a busy medical clinic, responsible for the schedules of six doctors and 15 people who serve as professional assistants or office support staff. On a Thursday afternoon, one of the doctors calls you and directs you to cancel his patients for the next day and to reschedule them for the following week. He offers no explanation, apology, or thanks, and you and your staff spend many hours to contact patients and rearrange the schedule.

What hot buttons can you identify?

_____

How do you feel about the doctor who called at the last minute?

_____

What explanation can you think of to explain the doctor's behavior?

_____

WHAT DID YOU LEARN?

Let's take a minute to summarize and reflect on this dimension, Actions of the Self.

1. **All emotions provide us with valuable information**, but some emotions can have negative consequences. Fortunately, we can learn to manage or modify them.

2. **Emotions are powerful and ubiquitous.** Emotions are present in your mind and imagination, in the home, in the workplace, in the political arena, and everywhere people are interacting around the globe. Emotions add to the richness of life!

3. **Our emotions are influenced by both internal and external factors.** Gaining an understanding of these various factors helps us understand why people have such different reactions to events or other people.

4. **We humans have many methods for managing our emotions** in order to feel good (happy, safe, balance, fulfilled--you choose your goal). This chapter provided some general guidelines for managing the feelings we don't especially like.

5. **Certain "hot buttons," when pushed, can lead to an "amygdale hijack"** and possibly to negative consequences for you and other people. You can learn ways to intervene, however, and to diminish the effect of the hot buttons.

6. **One technique for handling strong emotions such as anger or even rage is to replace them with curiosity**, a natural ability that we are all born with and can cultivate no matter what our age.

REFLECTION: ACTIONS OF THE SELF
ACTIONS OF THE SELF:

Individuals who are strong in this dimension:

- Are able to *manage* their own emotions
- Can *express* a range of feelings appropriately
- Are able to *plan* how to manage strong emotions in a given situation
- Have *developed ways to cope* with those emotions that are perceived to be "negative" and thus maintain their equilibrium

People are sometimes surprised to learn that they can successfully manage (not "control") even quite dramatic emotions such as anger, jealousy, and sadness.

BUILD ON SELF-AWARENESS

Being aware of your emotions—in the moment you are feeling them--is a great first step in learning to manage them. If you can identify what it is you are feeling, you can learn to acknowledge the emotion, understand how it may be expressed in your physiology, gain an understanding of why you feel that way, and plan a way to manage it if it involves negative consequences.

EXPLORING ACTIONS OF THE SELF

- Am I able to change my thoughts to change my emotions?
- Am I able to step back and see a difficult situation in perspective?
- When I experience "negative" emotions—such as during a conflict situation, can I retain my ability to reflect on what is happening?
- If I feel anxious in a situation, can I plan and implement steps to reduce my anxiety—including the use of humor?
- Can I use internal self-talk to take myself from a negative emotional state to a positive (or at least neutral) one?
- Am I able to use my anger in a given situation to be productive in, for example, problem solving?
- Can I give myself a "time out" for relaxation or reflection when the stress is mounting?
- Have I identified my "hot buttons" and found ways to manage my emotions when those buttons are pushed?

MAKE A PLAN TO IMPROVE

Reflect on the suggestions below that may be helpful in enhancing your skills in Actions of the Self. In the final chapter of this book, you will have an opportunity to choose activities for an Action Plan. At this point, all you need to do is think about whether any of these suggestions could be helpful to you in enhancing your actions of the self.

1. Rehearse how you will answer objections that you may face at an important meeting.
2. When you make a decision, check your "gut level" intuition against the facts of the situation.
3. Learn methods to calm yourself when you are angry or upset.
4. Make a conscious effort to listen more than you speak, and reflect on what may be different when you do so.
5. Practice managing your "hot buttons" so you can remain calm in stressful situations.
6. Conduct a personal survey of your routines and habits, and modify those that are ineffective, keeping track of your progress in a journal.
7. Do some reading or attend a workshop on how to use internal self-talk to take yourself from a negative emotional state to a positive one.

8. Pay attention to shifts in your physiology in response to people or events in your environment.

9. If public speaking, for example, fills you with fear, sign up for Toastmasters, or another course, to learn and practice public speaking.

10. Pay attention to the "stories" you make up about other people's behavior, and become more curious about why they are behaving in the way they do.

Four

Awareness of Others

BUILDING ON WHAT YOU'VE LEARNED

The first two dimensions of the Success Model were related to *intrapersonal* skills—being aware of your emotions and managing them in a variety of situations. Both self-awareness and self-management are lifelong skills, not something to be simply accomplished and set aside. But practice does make it easier to cope with the inevitable challenges that arise in a lifetime.

In this chapter, we move on to the *interpersonal* realm, that is, getting out of your own thoughts and feelings to become more aware of the feelings of others and to interact successfully with the people in your world—home, workplace, and community. Because of the wondrous and infinite variety in the people you know and meet, the skills involved in Awareness of Others are also skills to be practiced throughout our lives.

The Awareness of Others dimension includes specific skills and abilities that are necessary for the related dimension, Interaction with Others.

WHY IS THIS IMPORTANT?

Understanding how others are feeling—and having the ability to empathize with them—is the basis for building teams, complex organizations, and support networks in every area of our lives.

WHAT WILL YOU LEARN?

In this chapter, we'll explore two techniques that you can practice to enhance your ability to aware of others' emotions.

- Observation (facial expression, body language, other non-verbal communication)
- Active listening

Another essential skill that overlaps both Awareness of Others and Interaction with Others, is the ability to demonstrate empathy. We'll discuss empathy—why it is important and how to enhance your skills—in the next chapter (Interaction with Others).

I encourage you to look back at your self-assessment to take a look at your scores in this area.

Question for Reflection: How did you score on Awareness of Others on the assessment in Chapter 1?

_____

_____

In addition, you might ask yourself these questions:

1. How well do I observe other people to learn the feelings behind their words and actions?
2. How well am I able to really listen and understand what others are communicating?

_____

_____

_____

_____

DEFINITION: AWARENESS OF OTHERS

At the lower end of the range for this ability, individuals have a difficult time identifying and understanding what others are feeling whether through their words, actions, facial expressions, or body language. At the upper range are those individuals who are alert to what others are experiencing emotionally and are able to empathize with them.

The skill of listening to others—to the meaning of their words and to their intonation and voice volume--is a necessary aspect of awareness of others, but the ability to read how people are feeling by observing their facial expressions, their actions, and their body language is also part of such awareness.

If you are unable to "read" how others are reacting or feeling, you will find it more difficult to communicate, to influence others, and to build satisfying relationships and support networks.

EVERYDAY LIFE SCENARIOS

How do the skills (or the lack of skills) in Awareness of Others show up in our lives?

The people in the following scenarios show strong skills in the dimension:

SCENARIO: As Alonzo works with his daughter to teach her how to pitch a softball, he is alert to her facial expressions and body language to understand whether she understands him and whether she is feeling frustrated.

SCENARIO: Marisa becomes aware that whenever she and her husband mention their son's medical problems, their older daughter rolls her eyes and walks away from them.

The people in the following scenarios may need some development of skills in this dimension:

SCENARIO: Even at the end of a luncheon with friends, Edna seems oblivious to the fact that she has dominated the conversation with her complaints about one thing or another, and that a couple of people were mostly not participating and only giving each other silent looks.

SCENARIO: Lester, determined to get through all eleven of his talking points, never notices the annoyance on several faces as the meeting goes twenty-five minutes overtime.

Question for Reflection: Are there people you know who have similar strengths or lack of strengths?

_____

_____

_____

_____

_____

WHAT'S IN A FACE?

We become aware of others' emotions in several ways, some of them quite beneath our conscious awareness. One of the skills of this dimension is the ability to read the facial expressions of others. We begin learning this skill almost from the moment we are born.

If you've ever interacted with a baby, you are probably aware of how a baby studies your face and often mirrors your expressions. And actually, you mirror the baby's expressions too!

The eminent psychologist, Paul Ekman, has studied emotions for over 40 years. He has developed a system (the Facial Action Coding System or FACS), through which people can learn to read the "microexpressions" of some forty facial muscles. By employing the FACS system, you can learn to recognize when people are lying, but also to understand what they are feeling. Ekman and his team teach doctors, lawyers, law enforcement personnel, and performers to recognize these microexpressions, which can reveal "hidden" information about a person.

Dr. Ekman has established that there are seven universal expressions. No matter where you might go in the world, humans would have the same expression for these seven emotions. (Ekman even traveled to remote areas of the world where people had had little contact with the developed world and media. Even in these societies, he found that people had similar expressions for basic emotions.)

Question for Reflection: What seven emotions do you think would be recognizable by all human cultures? (No fair peeking at the answers at the bottom of the page.)

_____

_____

_____

_____

_____

Want to test yourself on recognizing these emotions? Go to http://www.cio.com/article/facial-expressions-test

Answers: Anger, Joy, Surprise, Fear, Sadness, Disgust, Contempt

TRY THIS AT HOME

Here's an experiential exercise that will demonstrate how we communicate through our facial expressions—our eyes, lips, eyebrows, and the many muscles of the face.

You can do this in front of a mirror to get the full effect. But even if you don't have a mirror handy, we think you'll find this exercise fun and informative.

For the following list of situations or events, say "Oh" to each situation, and observe the changes in your expression. (You can also try this with other words—"Interesting" or "Wow" but use the same word over and over.)

- Sunrise at a mountain campsite
- Fire visible on the upper story of a neighbor's home
- Holding a newborn baby minutes after the birth
- Receiving an unexpected check in the mail
- Seeing that the deer have nibbled your garden
- Called on the carpet by your boss
- The first taste of your favorite dish or dessert
- Facing a steep trail of switchbacks
- Awaking to the season's first snowfall
- Getting a flat tire as you are driving on a freeway
- Listening to a favorite piece of music on the radio
- Receiving a medical diagnosis of a serious health condition
- Being reunited with someone you love after a long absence

Question for Reflection: What observations did you make about your facial expressions as you said the same word to respond to different situations?

_____

_____

_____

_____

_____

SMILING IS CONTAGIOUS—AND GOOD FOR YOUR HEALTH

"When you smile you don't only appear to be more likable and courteous, you appear to be more competent."

--RON GUTMAN

We've talked about how contagious emotions are—but on particular facial expression, smiling, is shown to be not only contagious but significant in affecting our own emotions and well-being. Watch this video (see link below) and see what you think of this research on the power of smiling.

"Ron Gutman: The Hidden Power of Smiling TED Talk" (7:19 minutes)

https://www.ted.com/talks/ron_gutman_the_hidden_power_of_smiling

Question for Reflection: What reactions did you have to the video on smiling?

_____

_____

_____

_____

_____

BODY LANGUAGE AND OTHER NON-VERBAL COMMUNICATION

Facial expressions are just one aspect of non-verbal communication or body language. Whether you are actively speaking or quietly listening, you are communicating.

During election season, it has become popular to observe and analyze the body language of candidates. Analysts try to determine whether what the candidate says is matched in his or her non-verbal communication—gestures, eye contact, facial expressions, even the way a candidate shakes hands or makes physical contact with others.

"Experts" point out clues as to what message is being conveyed by these various forms of body language. But all of us are our own experts. We make these determinations, whether we are aware of them or not, at some level as we interact with others. We watch other people to understand whether we can trust them, be suspicious of them, or should avoid them.

Body language is just one way we are able to read the emotions of others—but it is a very important indicator of feelings/emotions.

You might be interested in watching a TED talk by Amy Cuddy, which presents the idea that body language affects how others see us, but it may also change how we see ourselves. Social psychologist Amy Cuddy shows how "power posing" — standing in a posture of confidence, even when we don't feel confident — can affect testosterone and cortisol levels in the brain, and might even have an impact on our chances for success.

"Your Body Language Shapes Who You Are" (21:02 minutes)

https://www.ted.com/talks/amy_cuddy_your_body_language_shapes_who_you_are

Resources:

The Complete Idiot's Guide to Body Language by Peter A. Andersen, Ph.D. The appendix to the book includes a thorough list of websites, books, and articles related to body language.

"Body Speaks: Body Language Around the World," Kris Rugsaken, www.nacada.ksu.edu/Resources/clearinghouse/View-Articles/body-speaks.aspx

BODY LANGUAGE IN THE HIRING PROCESS

In addition to the lead-up to political elections, another time when we become more aware of the importance of body language and non-verbal communication is during the hiring process—whether we are being interviewed or doing the interviewing. The significant information revealed in body language is the reason we rarely hire (or get hired) on just our written credentials and accomplishments.

What are the kinds of things we notice when we first meet someone?

- **Posture, body movement, stance:** We have a friend who claims to be able to identify anyone she knows simply by how they walk. In addition to a style of walking, people reveal themselves in how they carry themselves, how they sit or stand up, how they hold their head during a conversation.
- **Facial expression:** We've already talked about this one, so here's a quote to think about. It is from Ron Gutman, the same person who gave the TED talk on smiling (previous activity). "When you smile you don't only appear to be more likable and courteous, you appear to be more competent."
- **Eyes:** The eyes have been called "the windows of the soul." We can't say whether that is true, but certainly the eyes communicate a great deal—anger, attraction, interest, affection. We make eye contact with others to see how they are responding and to keep them in the flow of the conversation.
- **Space:** Unlike facial expressions, at least some of which can be understood universally, the amount of space that a person wants in relation to someone else differs with culture—as well as with the situation and the relationship of the two people. While it may be acceptable to stand close to an intimate friend, in other situations standing close could be interpreted as an aggressive act or an attempt to gain dominance.
- **Touch:** Again, cultural norms will vary, but the way we touch people can send very strong messages. Consider what you feel when someone shakes your hand firmly—or in a limp grip. Or consider a pat on the shoulder from your surgeon just before going into the operating room. Or a bear hug from a loved one. Or someone grabbing your arm when he or she disagrees with you. Or a pat on the head. Each touch gives us information.
- **Gestures:** Gestures can be easily misinterpreted when dealing with people from different cultures. Nevertheless, the way we point, raise our arms, wave, and use our hands when we are giving a speech or arguing with someone all provide signals about how we are feeling.
- **Voice:** How is it that you can pick up the telephone and recognize the speaker (if you've spoken before) from just a few words? We are quite adept at decoding voices—timing and pace, volume, tone and inflection, and the words we choose for agreement or understanding ("I see," "uh-huh," "got it.")

Question for Reflection: What body language stands out for you in an interview situation? Or what body language do you notice when first meeting someone?

_____

_____

_____

_____

ACTIVE LISTENING

Another skill that can be learned and can enhance your Awareness of Others is active listening. This refers to making a conscious effort during a conversation to:

- Carefully listen to the words of the other person
- Try to understand the whole message that the person is trying to convey

If you've ever had a tense conversation with a spouse, partner, friend, or child (and who has not?), you will recognize the fact that many of us are in the habit of not listening carefully and not really trying to understand what the person is feeling.

One of the best resources for learning this skill can be found on the MindTools website (www.mindtools.com). The following is excerpted from that site.

There are five key elements of active listening. They all help you ensure that you hear the other person, and that the other person knows you are hearing what they say.

1. PAY ATTENTION

Give the speaker your undivided attention, and acknowledge the message. Recognize that non-verbal communication also "speaks" loudly.

- Look at the speaker directly.
- Put aside distracting thoughts.
- Don't mentally prepare a rebuttal!
- Avoid being distracted by environmental factors. For example, side conversations.
- "Listen" to the speaker's body language.

2. SHOW THAT YOU'RE LISTENING

Use your own body language and gestures to convey your attention.

- Nod occasionally.
- Smile and use other facial expressions.
- Note your posture and make sure it is open and inviting.
- Encourage the speaker to continue with small verbal comments like "yes" and "uh huh".

3. PROVIDE FEEDBACK

Our personal filters, assumptions, judgments, and beliefs can distort what we hear. As a listener, your role is to understand what is being said. This may require you to reflect what is being said and ask questions.

- Reflect what has been said by paraphrasing. "What I'm hearing is . . .," and "Sounds like you are saying . . .," are great ways to reflect back.
- Ask questions to clarify certain points. "What do you mean when you say. . ." "Is this what you mean?"
- Summarize the speaker's comments periodically.

4. DEFER JUDGMENT

Interrupting is a waste of time. It frustrates the speaker and limits full understanding of the message.

- Allow the speaker to finish each point before asking questions.
- Don't interrupt with counter arguments.

5. RESPOND APPROPRIATELY

Active listening is a model for respect and understanding. You are gaining information and perspective. You add nothing by attacking the speaker or otherwise putting him or her down.

- Be candid, open, and honest in your response.
- Assert your opinions respectfully.
- Treat the other person in a way that you think he or she would want to be treated.

Question for Reflection: Is there someone in your life who has really listened to you? How did that make you feel?

_____

_____

_____

_____

_____

IF WE KNEW WHAT OTHERS WERE THINKING

What if we had the "superpower" to understand what is in the minds and hearts of the people we deal with every day? Would we treat people differently? Would it increase our empathy and our compassion? Watch this short video and see what you think.

"If We Could See Inside Others' Hearts" (4:44 minutes)

https://www.youtube.com/watch?v=Wl2_knlv_xw

Question for Reflection: Would you want this "superpower"—the ability to know how other people are feeling? Would it increase your compassion for them?

_____

_____

_____

_____

WHAT DID YOU LEARN?

Let's do a quick summary of the activities in this step on Awareness of Others.

1. Understanding how others are feeling—and having the ability to empathize with them—is the basis for building teams, complex organizations, and support networks.

2. At the lower end of the range for this ability, individuals have a difficult time identifying and understanding what others are feeling whether through their words, actions facial expressions, or body language. At the upper range are those individuals who are alert to what others are experiencing emotionally and are able to empathize with them.

3. Facial expressions are just one aspect of non-verbal communication or body language. Whether you are actively speaking or quietly listening, you are communicating.

4. The significant information revealed in body language is the reason we rarely hire (or get hired) on just our written credentials and accomplishments.

5. Active listening (carefully listening to the words of the other person and trying to understand the whole message that the person is trying to convey) is an important skill for enhancing Awareness of Others.

REFLECTION: AWARENESS OF OTHERS
AWARENESS OF OTHERS:

Individuals who are strong in this dimension:

- Are alert to what others are experiencing emotionally
- Are skilled in active listening
- Are able to read how people are feeling by observing their facial expressions and their body language
- Are able to feel empathy for others

If you are able to "read" how others are reacting or feeling, you will find it easier to communicate, to influence others, and to build satisfying relationships and support networks.

MAKE A PLAN TO IMPROVE

Reflect on the suggestions below that may be helpful in enhancing your skills in Awareness of Others. In the final chapter of this course, you will have an opportunity to choose activities for an action plan. At this point, all you need to do is think about whether any of these suggestions could be helpful to you in enhancing your awareness of others.

1. Do some reading or take a class on conflict management to improve listening skills.
2. Role-play another person's point of view in a situation where you disagree.
3. Sign up to volunteer to tutor at a local school or to stock shelves at a local food bank to gain a perspective on others' emotions.
4. Learn effective ways of delivering negative feedback or information.
5. Observe a colleague who appears to have a positive influence on the team, and try out some of his or her behaviors.
6. In both formal and informal settings, listen and ask questions to draw out your co-workers.
7. Once a month, go to lunch with one or more of your staff members to get to know their interests and goals in life.
8. Do some reading or go to a workshop to learn about understanding body language and facial expressions.
9. When someone disagrees with you, make a conscious effort to see the issue from his or her point of view before responding.
10. Ask yourself what personal bias you may have in a given situation.
11. Learn to read the emotions behind the words in your interactions with others.

Five

Interaction with Others

BUILDING ON WHAT YOU'VE LEARNED

Becoming more aware of our own emotions and the emotions of others is essential for creating satisfying and productive Interactions with Others, the fourth dimension of the Success Model of Emotional Intelligence. It is also an important skill for being able to act with compassion. Now that we've reached the fourth of the five dimensions of the Success Model, you are probably gaining a pretty good idea of how the dimensions overlap and build on each other.

Continuing to hone your skills in self-observation as well as observation of others will provide you with the tools needed to build strong relationships, teams, support networks, and healthy organizations. You will build on the skills of self-awareness and awareness of others to develop authentic connections with others—in your family, among your friends and colleagues, and in your community.

In this chapter, we'll explore:

- Empathy—the essential ingredient to developing sound relationships and compassion for others
- Interpersonal relationships in everyday life
- Enhancing interpersonal relationships and empathy

DEFINITION: INTERACTION WITH OTHERS

The ability to successfully interact with other people builds on your awareness of others' emotions. If you have well-developed skills in this dimension, you are able to utilize that awareness to build strong relationships, teams, and support networks. You are capable of empathy and compassion in interactions with other people, and you act with compassion when you become aware of another's pain.

Much of the success of Interaction with Others has to do with empathy—being able to place yourself in someone else's shoes and feel what that person is feeling. You are probably familiar with the idea of feeling empathy for a family member, close friend, or trusted colleague. You have experienced shared excitement, joy, pride, anger, and perhaps grief, just to name a few. But the concept of empathy has much wider implications for extending beyond your close circles to help you interact successfully with many different people—perhaps even strangers who happen to be in need of compassionate action.

EVERYDAY LIFE SCENARIOS

Think for a moment about the interactions you have at work. Even if you work mostly from home, chances are that you have conversations or meetings via telephone, and that you communicate via text and email. How would you rate the quality of the interactions in your workplace?

The workplace is sometimes described as a "minefield of interpersonal relationships." Leaders and managers devote a large percentage of their time to building relationships, resolving problems among employees, establishing trust, building collaborative teams, providing constructive feedback (and sometimes discipline), facilitating decision making, and making sure that people feel rewarded for a job well done.

But it is not just leaders and managers who must navigate the minefield of interpersonal relationships. Every person in the workplace—whether you work in a school, a factory, a restaurant, a shop, or an office--has to establish relationships with someone—or many someones. The crucial importance of establishing good relationships may seem obvious in some fields—healthcare, teaching, social services, and all kinds of sales for example. But even in less obvious situations—accounting, software development, or banking for example—strong interpersonal relationships are necessary for establishing a productive and satisfying environment.

So how do the skills (or lack of skills) in Interaction with Others show up in the workplace? The first two scenarios depict people who have strong skills in this dimension:

SCENARIO: When Charlene is publicly praised for completing a complex report on time, she immediately stands up, introduces her staff, and gives them credit for collaborating with her on the report.

SCENARIO: Jonathan calls his staff together after an announced merger and invites them to ask questions and discuss how the change in management and organizational structure might affect their jobs.

The next two scenarios depict people who could use some development in their Interaction with Others skills:

SCENARIO: When Javier's staff makes a case for postponing one of the strategies on his ambitious list of priorities, Javier refuses to even consider their ideas and tells them to stop complaining and get to work.

SCENARIO: When an employee fails to bring promised information to the meeting, Shari reminds him in front of his peers that the success of the team depends on each person doing his or her part on time.

Question for Reflection: Do you have people who match these skills—or lack of skills—in your workplace?

_____

_____

_____

_____

_____

SOCIAL ANIMALS

For most of us, the quality of our relationships—with family, friends, and colleagues—is a determining factor in how we feel about our lives. We don't want to feel that we are "alone." We want to feel connected. When our relationships are good, we feel good. When someone is angry with us or ignores us, we feel bad. We spend a great deal of energy engaged in doing things with or for those we love—spouses and partners, children, friends.

We even think up ways to do things together—from riding motorcycles to attending operas, from drinking at the local pub to cooking gourmet meals together, from exercising at the gym to participating in a 10K run to raise money for cancer research. We want to be *connected* to other people.

But why? What is it that makes us such "social animals?"

We human beings are not the only social animals of course. Most mammals, birds, and many insects can also be called social—rearing their young, living in groups (bigger than a family) and carrying out defined responsibilities for the good of the group.

We still have much to learn about the social interactions of non-human species—and about the interactions between humans and other animal species (how we love our pets!), but our focus here is on human interactions—on what occurs when we communicate in some way with other people.

Question for Reflection: How important is it for you to feel connected? How do you go about being connected in your life?

_____

_____

_____

_____

_____

BRAIN RESEARCH: MIRROR NEURONS AND EMPATHY

Recent and ongoing research in the neurosciences may help us understand this compelling need to interact with other human beings from the moment we emerge from the womb (or perhaps earlier) until we take our final breath. We teach each other and we learn from each other throughout our lifetimes. Brain research is one avenue for exploring how all this works.

I hope you took the time in chapter 1 to watch several short videos illustrating the contagion of emotions ("Laughing Babies Compilation," "T-Mobile Sing-Along," and "Christian the Lion"). If you want to watch or review the earlier videos, see "Experience Emotional Contagion for Yourself" in chapter 1 of this book.

The point of watching those videos was that we are all connected through the neurons of our brains, which are wired in a kind of "social superhighway," poised to interact with other people—in our homes, in the airport, in the mountains, in the classroom, in the boardroom, in the manufacturing shop—anywhere that people come together.

We're going to return to these mirror neurons, this time to understand more about the significance of our connection to others and how we can enhance these connections through empathy. Here is a link to a fascinating 7 minute video about mirror neurons and empathy:

"NOVA Science Now Mirror Neurons" (6:45 minutes)

https://www.youtube.com/watch?v=KA8xUayrLg

We see the possibility for further research to answer many questions about human interactions. For example:

- Why are we romantically drawn to certain individuals?
- Why are family or tribal or even country ties so strong?
- Can we improve our interactions with "strangers" so that they become friends?
- What implications might this research have for world peace?

Question for Reflection: Did this video prompt any questions in your mind?

_____

_____

INCREASING EMPATHY

Good news! Typically, if you are a generally stable person, your empathy has been increasing as you have grown older. If you reflect on your life, you will probably realize that your experiences, whether in "real life" or in reading about others, of new situations and of people who are different than you—in age, in gender, in skin color, in ability, in sexual orientation, in religious beliefs, in nationality—have increased your store of empathy. Once you can put an individual human face on one of these "differences," your empathy expands.

But there is more you can actually choose to do, actions you can take to increase your empathy and your ability to connect with family members, friends, colleagues, with bosses, and with those you interact with daily. Here is a brief list of possibilities:

- Make a habit of expressing your appreciation of others every day.
- Ask yourself, "What is this person feeling?" especially in those sticky situations.
- Be true to your promises to others.
- Become aware of the impact you have on others (keep a log!).
- Identify and support a project that provides service to others who are in need.
- Learn to listen by reflecting thoughts and feelings back to others.
- Read widely to include perspectives of others who live or have lived lives very different from yours.
- Ask gentle questions: What can I do for you? What do you need?
- Become an observer of how people express their feelings—including body language and other non-verbal communication.
- Build a work culture that is emotionally safe and friendly.
- Ask for feedback about your behavior, decisions, and words.
- Attempt to see a tough situation from another's perspective.
- Develop a sincere interest in other people by asking yourself what they have to teach you.
- Be willing to share your passions and interests with others.

Question for Reflection: Which one of these suggestions might be helpful to you in building empathy, compassion, and strong relationships with others?

THREE KINDS OF EMPATHY

The success of your interactions has much to do with empathy, but the concept of empathy is richer and more complex than presented so far.

As an example, imagine that a child—a toddler—has taken a fall on a cement sidewalk. You, the observer, may say to yourself something like, "Oh, that little girl seems to be unhappy. Maybe she has hurt herself." That is what psychologist Paul Ekman calls "cognitive empathy."

You might then be moved by that little girl's pain to remember your own pain or that of a loved one—in this case, remembering what it is like to have a scraped knee. That is "emotional empathy."

But what is it that makes us go a step further—like the people who put money in the blind man's cup (in the film referenced earlier)? What would make you stop and offer help to that man or to the child in this example? That is "compassionate empathy"—taking a step to actually do something for the person who is in pain—to reach out in some way to actually help.

Question for Reflection: What moves you to take a compassionate action? Can you think of an example?

_____

_____

_____

_____

EMPATHY ON THE WAY TO COMPASSION

A YouTube video that depicts a man feeding the poor in India is a good example of the three kinds of empathy: cognitive, emotional and compassionate.

"CNN Hero Narayanan Krishnan" (2:47 minutes)

https://www.youtube.com/watch?v=y_3BEwpv0dM

Question for Reflection: What reactions did you have to this man's compassionate acts?

_____

_____

_____

_____

_____

Resource: Akshaya Trust INDIA/Narayanan Krishnan

www.akshayatrust.org

NO MAN (OR WOMAN) IS AN ISLAND . . .

"No man is an island entire of itself; every man is a piece of the continent, a part of the main . . ."

The seventeenth-century poet John Donne wrote these words as part of a series of meditations as he was recovering from a life-threatening illness.

While a serious illness or some other life-altering event such as the loss of a loved one, a divorce, a move to a new city may make us pause and think about the profound importance of the other people in our lives, most of us are aware that our relationships have a lot to do with how happy or unhappy we are.

We know now that the ability to have good interactions with others helps define us as emotionally intelligent human beings. All models of Emotional Intelligence include this measure, but what can we do to enhance our interpersonal relationships?

BENEFITS OF STRONG INTERPERSONAL RELATIONSHIPS

Satisfying human relationships can greatly enhance the quality of our lives—and this is as true in the workplace as any other aspect of our lives. Although many of us spend a majority of our time in the workplace, we may not recognize the tremendous significance of our everyday interchanges with colleagues.

MASLOW'S HIERARCHY OF HUMAN NEEDS

Imagine the following as a pyramid with physiological needs at the base, and self actualization at the top.

SELF ACTUALIZATION

Morality, creativity, spontaneity, problem solving, lack of prejudice, acceptance of facts

ESTEEM

Self-esteem, confidence, achievement, respect for others, respect by others

LOVE/BELONGING

Friendship, family, sexual intimacy

SAFETY

Security of body, employment, resources, morality, the family, health, property

PHYSIOLOGICAL

Breathing, food, water, sex, sleep, homeostasis, excretion

In Abraham Maslow's hierarchy of human needs, acceptance and belongingness come right after the basic physiological and safety needs. When there is a culture of trust and openness in the workplace, executives, managers, and employees can all feel that they "belong," that they are accepted, and that their contribution is significant.

But there's more. When we feel that we are accepted and respected, we can gain inspiration and support among colleagues and friends. We can experience that distinctive enjoyment that results from being understood by another human being. And we can be pleasantly surprised at the result of interweaving our own ideas and perspectives with those of others.

SELF-ACTUALIZATION, CREATIVITY, AND INNOVATION

A sense of belonging is also necessary for a attaining a higher-level need—that of self-actualization, the ability of an individual to reach for and realize his or her potential. In today's workplace, collaboration and teamwork are highly valued. We know that working together often leads to greater productivity and the fulfillment of an organization's strategic objectives.

But perhaps more importantly, the sense of connection to others provides individuals with a solid footing that encourages them to be creative and innovative beyond mere expectations.

So what can we do to encourage better interpersonal relationships?

The following activities provide eight simple suggestions for increasing your ability to relate to others in a more satisfying way. If you are seeking to enhance this competency and to raise the level of your Emotional Intelligence, try out one or two of these with the people you interact with each day. Then just observe the effect that your action has on your interpersonal relationships.

SUGGESTION 1: SEEK TO INCREASE DIVERSITY.

No, this is not a new idea. As a nation, we've been working at this for many years, and the numbers of women, minorities, and other underrepresented groups in the workplace, in our schools, and in our communities have grown. But we sometimes forget just how limiting the old boy network was, and how easy it is to fall into hiring people who look and sound like ourselves. A true appreciation of diversity will include a broad spectrum of the categories we insist on placing people—gender, age, ethnicity, sexual orientation, culture, religion, political perspective, and educational background.

SUGGESTION 2: MAKE EACH COMMUNICATION MEANINGFUL.

John Donne would be astonished to know how many ways we have to communicate in the 21st century. As an observer of the human heart, however, he might not be so surprised to find that despite all our technological gadgets, we are still learning how to communicate in ways that truly connect us. Try thinking of each communication in your day—whether by telephone, email, an informal chat, a presentation at a formal meeting, or a conversation over coffee—as an opportunity to connect with another person. Recognize that emotions are the true currency of such communication.

SUGGESTION 3: BE CURIOUS.

Developing (or perhaps it is simply remembering) our inborn sense of curiosity about people, events, and objects can greatly increase our connections to others while also broadening and deepening our perspective about the world. Every person you meet has a story. Being curious about even a part of that story—what that person at the next desk is passionate about, where that person who cuts your hair went on vacation, how the hospitalization of a spouse or child has affected your neighbor—can result in increasing your own empathy but also in building strong connections and support networks.

SUGGESTION 4: EXPERIMENT WITH PROVIDING APPRECIATION, INTEREST, AND SERVICE.

Expressing your appreciation of even the more or less expected work of a family member or a colleague at work can result in much more than continued good work. The connections forged through demonstrating genuine interest or in performing acts of service for others are in themselves valuable. By becoming interested in others, you will create new pathways for the neurons in your own brain, enriching your satisfaction and your experience of the world.

SUGGESTION 5: SHARE AN EXPERIENCE THAT IS NOT WORK-RELATED.

A group of people can prepare and consume a meal together. Several people can team up to introduce ideas for recycling or promoting physical fitness. Plan a brown bag lunch in which one or more colleagues shares an interest outside of work—a passion for opera, or soccer, or bird watching, or travel, or a service organization's project. The possibilities for learning something are endless, and the connections you form with others by listening to them are perhaps even more valuable.

SUGGESTION 6: INVOLVE OTHERS IN DECISIONS.

While we may all be a bit cynical about the political polls that seem to be ubiquitous in the months before a major election, the idea of polling can help us recognize that the very act of asking people about their opinions can provoke them into thinking about an idea that they hadn't really considered. Asking people for their ideas and opinions, especially if they will experience the effects of a decision, can result in increased options, greater understanding of the issues, and enhanced interpersonal relationships. Of course, any decision must then be followed up with both appreciation and feedback.

SUGGESTION 7: PROVIDE A GIFT OF THE SENSES.

We are familiar with this idea in romantic relationships. We give flowers, candy, perfume—all intended to please the senses of the recipient. In the workplace, which is often a rather sterile environment, people appreciate those things that please their senses even in very small ways. With a bit of increased awareness, you can add pleasurable sensations that will be acknowledged at some level in others' brains. Such "gifts" can include a smile (vision), a few flowers from your garden (smell and vision), a plate of cookies (taste), a brief touch (oh yes, we have to be careful these days—but an appropriate touch on the arm or shoulder can be powerful), a genuine laugh, or a shared piece of music (hearing). All of these "gifts" will influence the recipients to experience positive feelings.

SUGGESTION 8: AVOID OR MINIMIZE REACTIONS TO THOSE WHO COMPLAIN, GOSSIP, ATTACK, BLAME, OR SUDDENLY EXPLODE.

It seems that every community has one or more of these characters. Some of them are family members or friends; some are in the workplace—they could be executives, managers, or employees—and all can be difficult in interactions. We've all wondered how best to deal with such people. It is worth repeating the truism here that it is not in our power to change them, but it is in our power to choose our reactions to them. One technique for changing our own reactions is to search for even a tiny bit of empathy for what that person is experiencing internally.

As John Donne knew way back in the seventeenth century, we are all connected. By increasing our ability to relate to each other, we contribute to a more emotionally intelligent world. Who will you connect with today?

Question for Reflection: Do any of these suggestions sound promising for enhancing your interpersonal relationships?

_____

_____

WHAT DID YOU LEARN?

Let's take a moment to summarize what we've learned in this step, Interaction with Others.

1. **Successful interactions are crucial** to building and maintaining a satisfied and productive team or support network.
2. **Humans are social animals**, and our brains are wired for social interaction and empathy.
3. We **can learn to increase the quality of our interactions** and our empathy for others and thus improve the quality of our lives.
4. **Empathy can become compassion**—with a wide reach and possible impact beyond our usual boundaries.

REFLECTION: INTERACTION WITH OTHERS

The ability to successfully interact with other people builds on an individual's awareness of others' emotions. An individual who is strong in this dimension utilizes that awareness to build strong relationships, teams, and support networks. Such an individual is capable of empathy and compassion in interactions with other people.

If you develop techniques for accurately evaluating the emotions of those with whom you interact, you will be less likely to make negative judgments and more likely to empathize—to put yourself in the shoes of those individuals—and to be able to develop relationships that are productive and satisfying. This ability is important for building successful teams and organizations as well.

MAKE A PLAN TO IMPROVE

Reflect on the suggestions below that may be helpful in enhancing your skills in Interactions with Others.

1. Consciously build relationships by asking others to join you in activities—lunch, a golf game, a poetry reading, a barbeque.
2. Share pictures of your family vacation, and encourage others to do the same.
3. Read a book or attend a workshop about how to manage interpersonal conflict.
4. Observe how a good role model handles difficult interpersonal situations, and experiment with his or her technique.
5. Work with a life or business coach to improve your interaction with customers.
6. Listen, *without judging*, as you plan a project with your colleagues.
7. Learn more about emotions in the workplace by reading, taking an online course, or attending a workshop.
8. Reinforce appropriate behavior by reacting positively.
9. Work with a coach to improve your supervisory skills.
10. Take an assessment of your Emotional Intelligence, and follow up by working with a coach to improve your skills.
11. Read a book about Emotional Intelligence in the workplace to help you in your job.
12. Reward your team with a catered lunch after a period of extra work.
13. Classify problems as technical, interpersonal, or a blend of the two to help you identify the best solution.
14. Become a role model for the kind of behavior you want to see in your family or team.

Six

Resilience

BUILDING ON WHAT YOU HAVE LEARNED

The Success Model includes Resilience as a significant aspect of Emotional Intelligence. Up to this point, we have considered two *intrapersonal* aspects of EI—Awareness of the Self and Actions of the Self, and two *interpersonal* dimensions--Awareness of Others and Interaction with Others. The multi-faceted concept of Resilience overlaps both the intrapersonal and the interpersonal. It is an exciting and complex concept!

Resilience may prove to be the most important dimension of EI. It contributes significantly to our sense of the meaning of life, to what makes life worthwhile.

It is the gentle, invisible hand at our back pushing us up the steep and difficult pathway. It makes use of humor, art and creativity, self-talk, and meditation to help us feel the infinitely varied and amazing moments of joy in our lives.

Resilience—actually the resilience of people—is also what fuels great teams and organizations, which are able to learn from the down times, the failures, and the setbacks to move forward toward greater success and fulfillment.

In this chapter, we will consider:

- The definition of resilience for individuals and organizations
- The importance of resilience to meet both everyday and extraordinary crises
- The science of resilience
- How to increase resilience

We only touch on the elements of Resilience in this book, but we encourage you to do more research and reading (you'll find suggestions on the Selected Resources in the appendix) on this fascinating subject.

DEFINITION: RESILIENCE

"In the midst of winter I finally learned there was in me an invincible summer."

--ALBERT CAMUS

Several factors such as optimism, flexibility, creativity, self-motivation, the ability to learn from mistakes and to recover from set-backs are significant aspects of Emotional Intelligence. In the Success Model, they are combined in a dimension called Resilience. It is resilience as much as any other aspect of EI that is the foundation for an individual's ability to maintain equilibrium and balance amidst inevitable changes and even crises that one encounters over a lifetime.

The American Psychological Associate defines resilience as "the process of adapting well in the face of adversity, trauma, tragedy, threats or even significant sources of threat." While our definition includes that adaptive process, we believe that resilience is crucial in meeting the challenges that confront us on a daily basis and that resilience can be enhanced and cultivated to create a rich, full life.

COPING WITH INTERNAL AND EXTERNAL CHALLENGES

Resilience is what fuels an individual's day-to-day motivation as he or she encounters *internal changes*—joy, sadness, boredom, love, intellectual curiosity, and anger to name just a few.

Resilience also helps us adapt to *external circumstances*, which include seasonal and weather changes, geographic re-locations, as well as emotionally charged environments in one's personal life or workplace. These inevitable changes as well as "Unexpected Life Events" (ULEs) are more successfully handled if an individual is flexible, optimistic, and prepared to cope with and learn from disappointments and setbacks. All of these abilities are aspects of resilience.

If we are resilient, we are also better equipped to reach out to those who are suffering or in pain. Resilience can keep us grounded, and provide us the strength to move forward in the face of huge challenges and even tragedy. In other words, from the reservoir of our own resilience, we can reach out with compassion for other beings.

EVERYDAY LIFE SCENARIOS

How do the skills of Resilience—or the lack of skills—show up in our lives?

Let's look first at two examples of people who have well-developed skills in resilience:

SCENARIO: When Lance looked at the C- on his paper, he wanted to walk out of the class and drop it immediately. He calmed himself a bit, put the paper away, and made a promise to himself to work harder than ever in the course and give it his best shot.

SCENARIO: Although Leah made it to the final round of interviews, she lost out to another candidate. After taking a couple days to recover and regain her confidence, she began applying to other positions.

What does it look like when people are lacking in resilience?

SCENARIO: After several months of trying to please his moody and demanding boss, Paul loses confidence in his own abilities, quits his job, and becomes so depressed that he is unable to even look for another job for several months.

SCENARIO: When she places fourth in the tennis tournament for the third time, Alice angrily blames the referees for bad calls, the hot weather for sapping her energy, and her opponents for having more time to practice. She decides to quit tournament play.

Question for Reflection: Do you recognize any of these strengths (or lack of strengths) in the people you know?

_____

_____

_____

_____

_____

WHY IS RESILIENCE IMPORTANT?

Imagine this: Disaster strikes—let's say a devastating hurricane followed by widespread flooding. Some people flee their flooded homes, some are stranded, and others are airlifted out or rescued by teams in boats. Past experience indicates that some of those people will become depressed and even suicidal. Others will bounce back and find the energy to reach out to others who need help, and they will have the energy to rebuild their lives.

What makes the difference in how people react to a bad situation? Is it possible to predict whether individuals and organizations will be resilient as they face difficulties, including problems that are not nearly as drastic as a hurricane.

Diane L. Coutu, a senior editor at Harvard Business Review, who wrote the article, "How Resilience Works" was interested in why some people suffer real hardships and do not falter. And why some organizations overcome seemingly insurmountable odds to prosper while other companies cave in at the slightest adversity.

Her research led her to conclude that resilient individuals—and resilient organizations—share three unique traits. Coutu says that you can bounce back from hardship with just one or two of these qualities, but you will only be truly resilient with all three:

- A resolute acceptance of reality
- A sense that life is meaningful
- An exceptional ability to improvise

Question for Reflection: Now, think of either an individual or an organization that has been confronted with a serious "unexpected life event," problem, or change. Did the person (or organization) demonstrate resilience? Did the individual (or organization) have one or more of the qualities that Diane Coutu lists as necessary?

_____

_____

_____

_____

_____

SCIENCE OF RESILIENCE

Fortunately, most of us will not have to face major catastrophes or extreme horrors during our lifetimes. But we can learn from studies of those who have suffered extreme psychological trauma—from child abuse, natural disasters, physical and sexual abuse, and from being exposed to the horrors of war.

Experts in these studies, Steven M. Southwick, M.D., and Dennis Charney, M.D. (authors of *Resilience: The Science of Mastering Life's Greatest Challenges*) wondered why some survivors were successful in overcoming adversity and bouncing back to live purposeful lives while others did not. They studied former prisoners of war, Special Forces instructors, and people who had endured horrific life traumas.

They recognized that some people were clearly more resilient than others, but resilience is not easy to pin down. It is the result of many factors—genetic, psychological, biological (and neurobiological), social, and spiritual. But it is not rare. If you think for a moment, you can probably name someone you know who has demonstrated resilience despite life's hard knocks.

WE CAN LEARN RESILIENCE

Here is the really good news: Southwick and Charney say that resilience is common and that *"everyone can learn and train to be more resilient."* The key, they point out, involves knowing how to harness stress and use it to our advantage.

Current and ongoing scientific research is providing evidence that *neurobiological systems associated with resilience can be strengthened to respond to stress*—through, for example, mindfulness meditation as well as "cognitive reappraisal," a method used by some psychotherapists.

Stress is actually necessary for growth. But the effect of the stresses of our 21ˢᵗ century world—cell phones, computers, six-lane freeways, nuclear weapons, the world population, and global climate change (just to name a few "new" stresses that our grandparents could not even imagine) are yet to be determined.

COPING WITH STRESS: SELF-TALK AND MEDITATION

Daniel Goleman, surely one of the most recognized experts in Emotional Intelligence studies, says that there are two ways to become more resilient: "one by talking to yourself, the other by retraining your brain."

We'll consider the idea of "talking to yourself" in another activity (on Martin Seligman and learned optimism), but for now, let's look at what Daniel Goleman has to say about "retraining your brain."

In his article, "Resilience for the Rest of Us" (*Harvard Business Review Blog Network*, April 25, 2011), Goleman explains what he means by retraining the brain. He provides an example of such training by Richard Davidson, a neuroscientist at the University of Wisconsin. Here are the instructions that were offered to the group being trained:

1. Find a quiet, private place where you can be undistracted for a few minutes—for instance, close your office door and mute your phone.
2. Sit comfortably, with your back straight but relaxed.
3. Focus your awareness on your breath, staying attentive to the sensations of the inhalation and exhalation, and start again on the next breath.
4. Do not judge your breathing or try to change it in any way.
5. See anything else that comes to mind as a distraction—thoughts, sounds, whatever—let them go and return your attention to your breath.

Many such studies report good results from mindfulness practice. Goleman says that to get the full benefit, a daily practice of 20 to 30 minutes works best. The jury may still be out on this, but studies in neuroscience are adding to our knowledge, and so far, the studies regarding meditation are promising for dealing with stress.

Question for Reflection: What are your thoughts about and experiences with meditation? Is it something you'd like to explore further?

_____

_____

_____

_____

_____

CULTIVATING POSITIVITY

"People say that what we're all seeking is a meaning for life. I think that what we're really seeking is an experience of being alive... so that we actually feel the rapture of being alive."

--JOSEPH CAMPBELL

Psychologist Barbara Fredrickson (author of *Positivity,* 2009) has spent much of her professional life examining "positive emotions," which she claims are worth cultivating. She defines "positive emotions". . ."from amusement to awe to interest to gratitude to inspiration—what they all have in common is that they are reactions to your current circumstances. They aren't a permanent state; they're feelings that come and go." But Fredrickson explains that they are also "wantable" states. She explains that "positive emotions have a kind of alluring glitter dust on them. You want to rearrange your day to get more of those sparkling moments."

In one study of positive emotions, reported in the *Journal of Personality and Social Psychology* (November, 2008), researchers measured the effects of loving-kindness meditation on people's resources. They concluded that the participants who learned to meditate did better on several measures of well-being, not because of learning to meditate, but because of the daily increase in positive emotions.

Dr. Fredrickson says that "over time positive emotions literally change who we are." According to Fredrickson, there are a number of benefits for people who increase their daily diet of positive emotions. They:

- Find more meaning and purpose in life
- Find that they receive more social support—or perhaps they just notice it more, because they're more attuned to the give-and-take between people
- Report fewer aches and pains, headaches, and other physical symptoms
- Show mindful awareness of the present moment and increased positive relations with others
- Feel more effective at what they do
- Are better able to savor the good things in life
- Can see more possible solutions to problems
- Sleep better

THE DIFFERENCES BETWEEN OPTIMISTS AND PESSIMISTS

People who are resilient are also optimistic. Psychologist Dr. Martin Seligman, author of *Learned Optimism: How to Change Your Mind and Your Life*, has studied optimism for almost three decades and is one of the proponents of Positive Psychology, an approach to studying human behavior that emphasizes the study of positive human functioning.

Seligman explains that optimists and pessimists suffer the same hard knocks in life. The difference is in how they explain the world to themselves—what Seligman calls their "explanatory style." This is important in the workplace because optimists are unfazed by defeat. When they are confronted by a bad situation, they perceive it as a challenge and try harder.

CONSIDER AN EXAMPLE:

Mark is a sales manager supervising a sales force of fifteen. Darlene is also a sales manager, and she supervises a similar size sales force but in a different region of the country. During the last six months, sales have fallen off sharply for both Mark and Darlene. As the following example demonstrates, their explanatory styles differ significantly. Mark is a pessimist. Darlene is an optimist.

PERMANENCE:

Darlene: We've recovered from a slump before. I know we can do it again.

Mark: Sales are spiraling downwards. We'll never recover from this.

PERVASIVENESS:

Darlene: Half of my team is still selling at or above the level of six months ago. We need to build on that.

Mark: Our overall statistics tell a dim story—we're sinking fast.

PERSONALIZATION:

Darlene: This is a result of the economy and the changes in market demand. It will change eventually.

Mark: This is my fault. I'm not fit to be a manager.

Question for Reflection: Where would you place yourself on a scale with pessimism at 0 and optimism at 10?

CAN YOU CHANGE YOUR EXPLANATORY STYLE?

This ABC exercise will guide you in changing your explanatory style if you choose to do so. First, let's summarize the difference in these styles:

Pessimists believe that bad events:

- Will last a long time
- Will undermine everything they do
- Are their own fault

Optimists believe that defeat or a bad event:

- Is just a temporary setback
- That its causes are confined to this one case
- That it is not their fault; circumstances, bad luck, or other people brought it about

The exercise has been adapted from Seligman's book, *Learned Optimism*. You'll have an opportunity to learn and practice the ABC technique for adapting your style to become more optimistic.

This technique can help you "change your feelings to change your mind." It consists of five steps:

1. **Adversity:** Write down whatever it is that you don't much want to do or something or someone that happened to cause you to react.
2. **Belief:** Write your thoughts about the annoyance or person (not your feelings, which will go under "consequences.")
3. **Consequences:** Record your feelings and what you did—how you reacted when the adversity happened.
4. **Disputation:** Argue with your own beliefs. Attack them as if they belonged to someone else. Think of any evidence you can that will dispute your beliefs.
5. **Energization:** If your "dispute" works, you should be able to go in a new direction with different feelings about the "adversity" that you face.

EXAMPLE:

Adversity: My section is falling behind its production schedules and my boss is beginning to complain about it.

Belief: Why can't the crew I've got do what they're supposed to do? I've shown them all they need to know, but they keep messing it up. Why can't I get them to work better? That's why I was hired. Now my boss is complaining. He thinks it's all my fault and I'm a lousy manager.

Consequences: I feel really angry and annoyed at my whole section, and I want to call them all into my office and chew them out. I also feel bad about myself and nervous about my job. I want to avoid my boss until we get back on schedule.

Disputation: First of all, it is true my section is falling behind. But I've got several new recruits, and it will take time for them to learn to do it right and work up to speed. I've had this before, but never with as many new guys. I've given them all the right instruction, but it still takes time. Some are quicker than others, and one is coming along really fast. I haven't done anything that's basically wrong. Also, the old hands are performing well, so it's just a matter of patience, and especially attention to the recruits. I've explained all this to my boss, and he knows it's true—he hasn't told me to try anything different. I'll bet he's under pressure from the production managers. They're not going to let up, so neither is he. I'll talk to him again and ask him directly if there's anything I've missed. At the same time, I'll keep working on the crew, motivating, encouraging, and pushing, and see if there's any way I can get the old hands to help.

Energization: I no longer feel like chewing them out. In fact, now I can discuss the situation with them calmly and with an open mind. I feel a lot less nervous about my job because I know I have a good record with the company. Also, instead of avoiding my boss, I will meet with him to give him a progress report and answer any questions he may have.

YOUR TURN TO ENERGIZE!
INSTRUCTIONS:

Each scenario below contains (A) an adversity or annoyance, (B) a set of beliefs about what happened, and (C) the consequences of your thoughts and feelings about the scenario.

Your challenge is to DISPUTE in order to ENERGIZE.

1. Read the scenario.
2. Write down whatever you can think of to dispute the beliefs and feelings.
3. Write the result of your dispute—how this person can go forward in a new direction with renewed energy.

SCENARIO 1

A. Adversity: About one minute into my presentation to the executive team, I realized that the links to the Internet in my PowerPoint presentation were not functional.

B. Belief: I rehearsed this presentation many times back at the office, and everything went perfectly. Now I look like an incompetent fool in front of the executive team. I can't even think about how to fix this quickly, so the whole presentation will be a flop.

C. Consequences: I feel so discouraged when I was hoping to impress the executive team. I can't even stand their politeness. It seems condescending. I know they think I'm an idiot, and I'll never get the promotion I've been working toward. I just want to go hide in my office.

D. Dispute:

_____

_____

_____

E: Energize:

_____

_____

_____

SCENARIO 2

A. Adversity: A long time client called to let me know he is switching to another supplier.

B. Belief: What did I do wrong? I have provided good customer service, and I've never heard any complaints. I must have done something to make him dislike me.

C. Consequences: I feel terrible about myself, and to tell the truth, I feel really angry at this client. He has some nerve just cancelling after I've given him good customer service for a long time. What if I lose another major client? What if I'm losing my touch? This is going to make me look bad, and I could lose other clients as well.

D. Dispute:

_____

_____

_____

E: Energize:

_____

_____

_____

SITUATION 3

A. Adversity: My boss called me in to tell me that my division's budget will be cut by 15 percent for this next year.

B. Belief: My boss doesn't think I'm a good leader. He doesn't agree with the direction I was taking my division. A 15 percent cut will stop our progress and may even mean that we go backwards.

C. Consequences: I feel that I'm being treated unfairly by my boss. Just because I don't go flattering her and making empty chitchat, she is favoring other divisions over mine. Others are jealous of my division's record and have probably complained to her behind my back. This budget cut will have negative consequences for our division, and I'll probably end up losing my job.

D. Dispute:

_____

_____

_____

_____

E: Energize:

_____

_____

_____

_____

LEARN OR DO SOMETHING NEW—THE CHALLENGE

"You may grow old and trembling in your anatomies, you may lie awake at night listening to the disorder of your veins, you may miss your only love, you may see the world about you devastated by evil lunatics, or know your honour trampled in the sewers of baser minds. There is only one thing for it then – to learn. Learn why the world wags and what wags it. That is the only thing which the mind can never exhaust, never alienate, never be tortured by, never fear or distrust, and never dream of regretting. Learning is the thing for you."

--T.H. WHITE

Expected life spans have been increasing around the globe. What will help us build and maintain resiliency through our working years and beyond? I believe that lifelong learning is the key to resiliency at any age. Here are a few suggestions for learning or doing something new every week.

1. EMBRACE CHALLENGES

You can learn from challenges—those that you think up for yourself but also those challenges that disrupt our lives as Unexpected Life Events. Challenges can range from dealing with a difficult boss to cutting 20% from your department budget. It could also be a challenge in your personal life—caring for an aging parent or an unexpected medical issue of your own. If you have a new challenge this week—welcome it as an opportunity to learn something new and to become more resilient.

2. INTERACT WITH PEOPLE--AND ANIMALS TOO!

It's great to have your familiar friends and family who support you, but stretching yourself to meet new people or even to pay attention to your pet animals can greatly enhance your resilience.

3. OBSERVE THE NATURAL WORLD WITH ALL YOUR SENSES.

And what can be better for increasing resilience than getting out into the natural world and using your senses to explore and learn. Whether you take a five-day backpacking trip or do ten minutes of weeding in your own backyard, there are great lessons waiting to be learned.

4. SEEK TO UNDERSTAND HOW SOMETHING WORKS--BE CURIOUS.

When my son Peter was three years old, he asked me whether helicopters have wheels. I had no idea how to answer him—though I've learned since that some do and some don't and that you can jack up the ones that don't and put wheels under them to move the helicopter—but I'll never forget the curiosity that my small son reintroduced me to. Being curious about how the world works can help increase your knowledge—and your resilience.

5. READ!

I'm absolutely sold on reading as a way to gain knowledge, to learn empathy from others' emotions and experiences, and even as a constructive escape when the world looks bleak. In reading, you can travel to the arctic, to a tropical island, backwards in time, or to a distant planet light years from now. You can experience hardship without actual suffering and learn what others have gained from those experiences. Reading something new every week is one of the easiest ways to "learn or do" something new—and one of the best methods we know for building resilience. [*Resource* - "Your Brain on Fiction" by Annie Murphy Paul in *The New York Times*, March 17, 2012]

6. DO SOMETHING YOU'VE NEVER DONE BEFORE--OR DO IT DIFFERENTLY.

What haven't you done that you'd like to try? But you don't have to sign up for a class or spend money to travel half way around the world. This can be as simple as taking a new route to work—or perhaps riding a bike to work, or treating your office mates to fresh pastries or pizza, or sitting in a coffee shop as you create your next business proposal. The idea is simply to do something new or in a new way and see what happens. It's up to you and—the sky's the limit!

So here's the challenge! Get out a calendar where you can keep track—and learn or do something new every week. Make it a habit, and I'm betting that you'll not only have fun but you will build your resilience toward becoming a more emotionally intelligent human being.

Question for Reflection: What will you learn or do to enhance your resilience this week?

_____

_____

_____

_____

_____

_____

CREATIVITY AND PROBLEM SOLVING

Many organizations—from educational institutions to software development and biomedical technology companies—are looking for employees who are creative and innovative. The ability to be creative—to imagine possibilities to put things together in new ways, and to come up with new approaches to old problems—is valuable in all aspects of our society.

DeWitt Jones is a photographer for National Geographic as well as an author and motivational speaker. In one short video he explains his approach to taking a photograph. With each shot he says that the picture is "another right answer."

His point is that there are "many right answers" and many perspectives to explore. Such creativity strengthens resilience and contributes to greater health, satisfaction, and success. It is an attitude we can all learn to cultivate.

You may be interested in watching the inspiring video of DeWitt Jones at this link:

"DeWitt Jones on Creativity" (6:25 minutes)

https://www.youtube.com/watch?v=tqF_D5GkrAo

Question for Reflection: How might your creativity contribute to your resilience?

_____

_____

_____

_____

_____

HUMOR

"Humor is just another defense against the universe."

--MEL BROOKS

I hope you are not expecting some hilarious jokes here. Personally, I do find any number of jokes, situations, and stories to be humorous, but I know from experience that not everything I find funny will be considered funny by you or anyone else!

For example . . . do you find any of the following laugh-out-loud-funny?

1. A squirrel is a rodent with good PR.
2. When Jackie Kennedy was diagnosed with lymphoma, she remarked that if she had know this would happen, she wouldn't have done all those sit-ups.
3. *Candid Camera* set-up: A woman is at the side of the road with her car—obviously in some difficulty. When a guy pulls over to help, he lifts the hood of the car only to find that there is nothing—no engine, nothing—under the hood. The woman plays innocent and ignorant.

I have found all of these quite humorous, a fact that may surprise you if you think they're just kind of dumb or silly. Humor, of course, is often related to context. At my home, we have long fought the cute little squirrels who attempt to dump our birdfeeders and are quite smart at outsmarting us. We have also experienced the overwhelming diagnosis of cancer and found Jackie Kennedy's remark hilarious. And the *Candid Camera* episode is a very old one, but it never fails to provide me with giggles.

Our point is that having a good sense of humor is a gift and that it can be helpful in building resilience.

Question for Reflection: Can you think of a time when humor helped you in a stressful situation?

_____

_____

_____

_____

_____

_____

GRATITUDE COUNTS
Count your blessings.

We've all heard this simple sentence or something like it since we were children. In an inspiring TED talk by photographer Louie Schwartzberg, he says the same thing with a bit more eloquence. I offer a link to it here with the hope that it will inspire you as you continue journey toward greater Emotional Intelligence.

Louis Schwartzberg: Nature. Beauty. Gratitude (9:39 minutes)

https://www.youtube.com/watch?v=8IXYZ6s3Dfk

Question for Reflection: Did this video prompt feelings of gratitude in you?

_____

_____

_____

_____

WHAT DID YOU LEARN?

Let's review a few points about Resilience.

1. Resilience may prove to be the most important dimension of Emotional Intelligence. It contributes significantly to our sense of the meaning of life, to what makes life worthwhile. It is also the essential ingredient for coping with what I like to call Unexpected Life Events, or ULEs.

2. Several factors such as optimism, flexibility, creativity, self-motivation, the ability to learn from mistakes and to recover from setbacks are significant aspects of Emotional Intelligence. It is resilience as much as any other aspect of EI that is the foundation for an individual's ability to maintain equilibrium and balance amidst inevitable changes and even crises that one encounters over a lifetime.

3. According to Diane L. Coutu, a senior editor at *Harvard Business Review*, resilient individuals—and resilient organizations—share three unique traits.

4. According to researchers and authors Steven M. Southwick, M.D. and Dennis Charney, M.D., resilience is common and "everyone can learn and train to be more resilient." The key involves knowing how to harness stress and use it to our advantage.

5. Daniel Goleman says that there are two ways to become more resilient: "one by talking to yourself, the other by retraining your brain."

6. Researcher Dr. Barbara Fredrickson says that "over time positive emotions literally change who we are." There are a number of benefits for people who increase their daily diet of positive emotions.

7. Dr. Martin Seligman explains that optimists and pessimists suffer the same hard knocks in life. The difference is in how they explain the world to themselves—what Seligman calls their "explanatory style," which can be changed.

8. Lifelong learning—"learn or do something new every week"—is a key aspect of resiliency at any age.

9. Creativity and a sense of humor are also key aspects of resiliency.

10. Cultivating an attitude of gratitude counts in enhancing resiliency.

REFLECTION: RESILIENCE

Resilience is a significant factor in the make-up of the emotionally intelligent individual. This dimension is what fuels an individual's day-to-day motivation as he or she encounters internal changes—joy, sadness, boredom, love, intellectual curiosity, and anger to name just a few—as well as external changes that run the gamut from seasonal and weather changes to geographic re-locations to emotionally charged environments in one's personal life or workplace. These inevitable changes are more successfully handled if an individual is flexible, optimistic, and prepared to cope with and learn from disappointments and setbacks. All of these abilities are aspects of resilience.

MAKE A PLAN TO IMPROVE

Reflect on the suggestions below that may be helpful in enhancing your skills in Resilience. In the final chapter of this book, you will have an opportunity to choose activities for an action plan. At this point, all you need to do is think about whether any of these suggestions could be helpful to you in enhancing your resilience.

1. Take a 20-minute walk twice a day, do yoga, or meditate to relieve stress.
2. On the weekend, take a hike in the mountains with a family member or friend.
3. Take an online course in time management skills.
4. Plan a 3-minute worry break for later in the day.
5. Take an online course in "improving your self talk" to be more positive.
6. Resurrect an old interest (e.g., singing, bird watching, dancing, photography), and take a class to get back into it.
7. Take a walk at lunch time each day (in any kind of weather) to feel healthier and less stressed.
8. Begin each day with a half-hour of quiet reflection and goal setting.
9. Take the lead in planning a family or friends reunion.
10. Start a project or activity you've been meaning to do for years.
11. At the end of a busy week, watch a couple of comedies that you anticipate will make you laugh out loud.
12. Learn the ABC technique ("change your thinking to change your feelings") to deal with your emotional reactions to unpleasant or upsetting events and improve your optimism.
13. Build a support team that will provide honest feedback in a supportive and positive manner.
14. Learn and implement a system to become more organized and less stressed.

Seven

Create An Action Plan

CAN EMOTIONAL INTELLIGENCE MAKE A DIFFERENCE?

Emotional Intelligence is not a new concept. It did not begin with Dan Goleman's book in 1995 or the work of any other twentieth century researchers, although we can thank these individuals for giving it a name, describing it, and attempting to measure it.

Emotionally intelligent people have existed probably since humankind began, and we can likely find elements of EI in some animals. We can look far into human history to find examples of people who had strong emotional intelligence and those who lacked such skills or used them for unethical ends.

Reviewing some of the concepts we've covered in this book, we've learned that Emotional Intelligence skills can:

- Create more harmonious families
- Improve your odds of gaining a job
- Foster better relationships, teams and organizations
- Lead to less stress and better health
- Build support networks to assist you in times of need
- Help you move up the career ladder
- Increase your strength to meet challenges and inevitable losses
- Free you to become more innovative, creative, and resilient

Question for Reflection: How will you implement the skills of Emotional Intelligence?

_____

_____

_____

_____

EMOTIONAL INTELLIGENCE FOR A MORE COMPASSIONATE WORLD

While all of benefits listed on the previous page may indeed grow out of greater Emotional Intelligence, we think there is a much more significant outcome.

Emotional Intelligence skills and competencies can become the fertile ground for a *more compassionate world*. The skills that contribute to the various components of EI—self-awareness, self-management, awareness of and interaction with others, and resilience— may be viewed as prerequisites to the development of compassion in individuals, in families, in the workplace, in communities, and in the interconnected societies of people throughout the world.

Compassion is a concept that is deeply embedded in our human consciousness. We can consider the meaning and origins of the word "compassion" in various languages. We can read about the concept in discussions of ethics and morality. We can take into account the stories, parables, and theologies of various world religions. And we can read about compassion in the context of various related qualities and concepts in academic journals as well as popular magazines, articles, and videos.

A relatively recent approach to understanding compassion comes from scientific research. I will propose here a practical definition (a combination of definitions from the Greater Good Science Center based at the University of California, Berkeley and that of Dan Martin, a professor and researcher in social psychology and business management at California State University, East Bay):

> *Compassion is a feeling that arises when a person becomes aware of another's suffering, feels empathy for that person, and takes action to ameliorate that suffering.*

Resource: "Being Compassionate," Section 2 of Chapter 28, Spirituality and Community Building, Community Tool Box, University of Kansas:

http://ctb.ku.edu/en/table-of-contents/spirituality-and-community-building/being-compassionate/main

BUT WHAT CAN ONE PERSON DO?

While individual acts of compassion are to be encouraged, often they may not be enough to influence long-standing, entrenched, and emotionally-laden issues within a community—gang violence, drug use, domestic violence, police brutality, homelessness, racial injustice, human trafficking, chronic hunger, and prejudice against immigrants. Even those of us who feel great compassion around these issues may feel powerless and perhaps hopeless in trying to resolve them on an individual basis.

In their book *Connected: The Surprising Power of Our Social Networks and How They Shape Our Lives*, renowned scientists Nicholas Christakis and James Fowler use the metaphor of the "bucket brigade" to emphasize the increased effectiveness of people working in connected networks as opposed to the same number of people working as individuals. For example, if a house is burning and a hundred people (who happen to have buckets) carry buckets back and forth from the river to douse the fire, they will be ten times less effective in putting out the fire than a line of people passing buckets of water from the river to the fire.

Question for Reflection: Can you imagine a "bucket brigade" for bringing greater compassion to the world we share with over 7 billion people?

_____

_____

_____

_____

IMAGINE . . .

Here is one beautiful example of people working together—the Charter for Compassion International (CCI).

CCI has been building a "network of networks"—a more complex version of the bucket brigade--to connect individuals, organizations, and institutions, as well as several hundred compassionate communities worldwide, which are already making compassion their focus and motivating force.

The Charter for Compassion International envisions a world in which compassion and compassionate action, as articulated in the Charter, will become a transformative energy, motivating individuals and communities to care for each other, to relieve suffering wherever it is found, and to connect to other communities across the globe to ensure well-being for all beings on the planet.

CCI is an organization inspired by author and religious historian Karen Armstrong, who won the $100,000 TED prize for her wish to create, launch, and propagate a global compassion movement based on the golden rule. She worked with a group of scholars and religious leaders from all over the world to write what is now known as the Charter for Compassion (http://charterforcompassion. org/the-charter), launched in 2009. The Charter has inspired many thousands of individuals, who have signed on to it and have committed themselves to "make compassion a clear, luminous, and dynamic force" toward creating a "peaceful global community."

CCI invites and welcomes individuals, groups and organizations, and communities of all sizes to sign the Charter (http://charterforcompassion.org/sign-share-charter) and join in working for a more compassionate world—perhaps by working to transform your own community into a Compassionate Community (http://charterforcompassion.org/communities). The organization's vision is to connect individuals, organizations, and institutions that are working to make compassion central to their daily activities in their own communities toward realizing its global vision.

Want to learn more? Please visit the CCI website http://www.charterforcompassion.org

THE CHARTER FOR COMPASSION

The principle of compassion lies at the heart of all religious, ethical and spiritual traditions, calling us always to treat all others as we wish to be treated ourselves. Compassion impels us to work tirelessly to alleviate the suffering of our fellow creatures, to dethrone ourselves from the centre of our world and put another there, and to honour the inviolable sanctity of every single human being, treating everybody, without exception, with absolute justice, equity and respect.

It is also necessary in both public and private life to refrain consistently and empathically from inflicting pain. To act or speak violently out of spite, chauvinism, or self-interest, to impoverish, exploit or deny basic rights to anybody, and to incite hatred by denigrating others—even our enemies—is a denial of our common humanity. We acknowledge that we have failed to live compassionately and that some have even increased the sum of human misery in the name of religion.

We therefore call upon all men and women to restore compassion to the centre of morality and religion ~ to return to the ancient principle that any interpretation of scripture that breeds violence, hatred or disdain is illegitimate ~ to ensure that youth are given accurate and respectful information about other traditions, religions and cultures ~ to encourage a positive appreciation of cultural and religious diversity ~ to cultivate an informed empathy with the suffering of all human beings—even those regarded as enemies.

We urgently need to make compassion a clear, luminous and dynamic force in our polarized world. Rooted in a principled determination to transcend selfishness, compassion can break down political, dogmatic, ideological and religious boundaries. Born of our deep interdependence, compassion is essential to human relationships and to a fulfilled humanity. It is the path to enlightenment, and indispensable to the creation of a just economy and a peaceful global community.

ACTION PLAN FOR ENHANCING YOUR EMOTIONAL INTELLIGENCE

This Action Plan will guide you through the process of reviewing, reflecting, and then looking forward to practicing some of the skills that will help you increase your skills in the dimensions of Emotional Intelligence.

Take some time to review the "Reflection" pages that you worked on at the end of each chapter.

Next, write down your scores (below) from the assessment you took in Chapter 1. This may help you think about where to begin your action planning.

Emotional Intelligence Scores: Write your assessment scores here.

- Awareness of the Self   _____
- Actions of the Self   _____
- Awareness of Others   _____
- Interaction with Others   _____
- Resilience   _____

Don't try to do too much at once—take just a few small steps. Then ask yourself: *What one or two action steps can I commit to in the next two weeks for improving my Emotional Intelligence?*

Each of the five sections below (which correspond to the five dimensions of the Success Model) includes a brief review and then a list of suggested action steps you can take to enhance your EI skills.

AWARENESS OF THE SELF

"It is better to conquer yourself than to win a thousand battles. Then the victory is yours. It cannot be taken from you, not by angels or by demons, heaven or hell."

---BUDDHA, 568-488

QUICK REVIEW

Self-awareness is the foundational building block of Emotional Intelligence. The first step in enhancing or building your overall Emotional Intelligence is achieving a healthy level of self-awareness—which is the ability to identify emotions in the self and to perceive the impact you have on others at home, in the workplace, within the local community, and beyond that if you happen to have a wider sphere of influence.

More specifically, being self-aware means that you can:

- Identify your own feelings
- Recognize how people perceive you
- Recognize how you respond to people in a variety of situations
- Identify your intent and attitude as you communicate with others

Increasing your ability to observe—both yourself and others—will enhance your Emotional Intelligence. You can practice these skills in your own reflections, in your everyday interactions with others, or even when you watch TV or a movie.

For increased self-awareness, get in the habit of asking yourself:

- What am I feeling as I (interact, listen, speak, make a presentation, etc.)?
- What would this person (or these people) say or feel about me when I've left the room?
- What is my intent as I (interact, listen, speak, make a presentation, etc.)?
- What am I revealing about how I feel in my facial expressions, my body language, and my style of dress?
- What can I do to better make the impact that I intend and to convey my message?

CREATE YOUR PLAN

Use a pen or a highlighter to choose one or two actions you can commit to today.

1. Take time to list your values (what matters most to you) for the next "chapter" of your life.
2. After a difficult personal encounter (boss, spouse, child, friend, stranger), analyze what you are feeling.
3. Hire a "shadow coach" to give you feedback on your time management, your productivity, or your interactions with colleagues.
4. Be aware of when you are thinking negative thoughts. Keep track.
5. Survey your strengths and plan to consciously use them more on a daily basis.
6. Ask a trusted colleague to observe you in meetings and give you honest feedback about your interactions, your facial expressions, your body language, and your influence on the group.

7. In decision-making sessions with your co-workers, make it a habit to ask, "What might be the unintended consequences of this action?"
8. Take a 360-degree feedback survey with your colleagues, boss, and direct reports.
9. Keep track of situations that make you angry or upset, situations that make you feel pleased and happy, and identify the emotions you are feeling.
10. Observe the impact that your words and behaviors—both "positive" and "negative"--have on others. (Begin with one person or a small team.)
11. Take an assessment of your Emotional Intelligence, and follow up by working with a coach to improve your skills.

ACTIONS OF THE SELF

"Fear less, hope more, eat less, chew more, whine less, breathe more, talk less, say more, hate less, love more; all good things will be yours."

--SWEDISH PROVERB

QUICK REVIEW

Individuals who are strong in this dimension:

- Are able to manage their own emotions
- Can express a range of feelings appropriately
- Are able to plan how to manage strong emotions in a given situation
- Have developed ways to cope with those emotions that are perceived to be "negative" and thus maintain their equilibrium

People are sometimes surprised to learn that they can successfully manage (not "control") even quite dramatic emotions such as anger, jealousy, and sadness.

Being aware of your emotions—in in the moment you are feeling them--is a great first step in learning to manage them. If you can identify what it is you are feeling, you can learn to acknowledge the emotion, understand how it may be expressed in your physiology, gain an understanding of why you feel that way, and plan a way to *manage* it if it involves negative consequences.

CREATE YOUR PLAN

Use a pen or a highlighter to choose one or two actions you can commit to today.

1. Rehearse how you will answer objections that you may face at an important meeting.
2. When you make a decision, check your "gut level" intuition against the facts of the situation.
3. Learn methods to calm yourself when you are angry or upset.
4. Make a conscious effort to listen more than you speak, and reflect on what may be different when you do so.
5. Practice managing your "hot buttons" so you can remain calm in stressful situations.
6. Conduct a personal survey of your routines and habits, and modify those that are ineffective, keeping track of your progress in a journal.
7. Do some reading or attend a workshop on how to use internal self-talk to take yourself from a negative emotional state to a positive one.
8. Pay attention to shifts in your physiology in response to people or events in your environment.
9. If public speaking, for example, fills you with fear, sign up for Toastmasters, or another course, to learn and practice public speaking.
10. Pay attention to the "stories" you make up about other people's behavior, and become more curious about why they are behaving in the way they do.

AWARENESS OF OTHERS

"Kindness is in our power, even when fondness is not."

-SAMUEL JOHNSON (1709-1784)

QUICK REVIEW:

Individuals who are strong in this dimension

- Are alert to what others are experiencing emotionally
- Are skilled in active listening
- Are able to read how people are feeling by observing their facial expressions and their body language
- Are able to feel empathy for others

If you are able to "read" how others are reacting or feeling, you will find it easier to communicate, to influence others, and to build satisfying relationships and support networks.

CREATE YOUR PLAN

Use a pen or a highlighter to choose one or two actions you can commit to today.

1. Do some reading or take a class on conflict management to improve listening skills.
2. Role-play another person's point of view in a situation where you disagree.
3. Sign up to volunteer to tutor at a local school or to stock shelves at a local food bank to gain a perspective on others' emotions.
4. Learn effective ways of delivering negative feedback or information.
5. Observe a colleague who appears to have a positive influence on others, and try out some of his or her behaviors.
6. In both formal and informal settings, listen and ask questions to draw out others.
7. Once a month, go to lunch with one or more of your staff members to get to know their interests and goals in life.
8. Do some reading or go to a workshop to learn about understanding body language and facial expressions.
9. When someone disagrees with you, make a conscious effort to see the issue from his or her point of view before responding.
10. Ask yourself what personal bias you may have in a given situation.
11. Learn to read the emotions behind the words in your interactions with others.

INTERACTION WITH OTHERS

"You can discover more about a person in an hour of play than in a year of discussion."

--PLATO, PHILOSOPHER (427-347 BCE

QUICK REVIEW

The ability to successfully interact with other people builds on an individual's awareness of others' emotions. An individual who is strong in this dimension utilizes that awareness to build strong relationships, teams, and support networks. Such an individual is capable of empathy and compassion in interactions with other people.

If you develop techniques for accurately evaluating the emotions of those with whom you interact, you will be less likely to make negative judgments and more likely to empathize—to put yourself in the shoes of those individuals—and to be able to develop relationships that are productive and satisfying. This ability is important for building successful teams, organizations and support networks.

CREATE YOUR PLAN

Use a pen or a highlighter to choose one or two actions you can commit to today.

1. Consciously build relationships by asking others to join you in activities—lunch, a golf game, a poetry reading, a barbeque.
2. Share pictures of your family vacation, and encourage others to do the same.
3. Read a book or attend a workshop about how to manage interpersonal conflict.
4. Observe how a good role model handles difficult interpersonal situations, and experiment with his or her technique.
5. Work with a life or business coach to improve your interaction with customers.
6. Listen, without judging, as you plan a project with your colleagues.
7. Learn more about emotions in the workplace by reading, taking an online course, or attending a workshop.
8. Reinforce appropriate behavior by reacting positively.
9. Work with a coach to improve your supervisory skills.
10. Take an assessment of your Emotional Intelligence, and follow up by working with a coach to improve your skills.
11. Read a book about Emotional Intelligence in the workplace to help you in your job.
12. Reward your team with a catered lunch after a period of extra work.
13. Classify problems as technical, interpersonal, or a blend of the two to help you identify the best solution.
14. Become a role model for the kind of behavior you want to see in your family or team.

RESILIENCE

"Be content with what you have, rejoice in the way things are. When you realize there is nothing lacking, the whole world belongs to you."

--LAO TZU

QUICK REVIEW

Resilience may prove to be the most important dimension of Emotional Intelligence. It contributes significantly to our sense of the meaning of life, to what makes life worthwhile. It is also the essential ingredient for coping with what we like to call Unexpected Life Events, or ULEs.

Several factors such as optimism, flexibility, creativity, self-motivation, the ability to learn from mistakes and to recover from setbacks are significant aspects of Emotional Intelligence. It is resilience as much as any other aspect of EI that is the foundation for an individual's ability to maintain equilibrium and balance amidst inevitable changes and even crises that one encounters over a lifetime.

This dimension is what fuels an individual's day-to-day motivation as he or she encounters internal changes—joy, sadness, boredom, love, intellectual curiosity, and anger to name just a few—as well as external changes that run the gambit from seasonal and weather changes to geographic re-locations to emotionally charged environments in one's personal life or workplace.

These inevitable changes are more successfully handled if an individual is flexible, optimistic, and prepared to cope with and learn from disappointments and setbacks. All of these abilities are aspects of resilience.

CREATE YOUR PLAN

Use a pen or a highlighter to choose one or two actions you can commit to today.

1. Take a 20-minute walk twice a day, do yoga, or meditate to relieve stress.
2. On the weekend, take a hike in the mountains with a family member or friend.
3. Take an online course in time management skills.
4. Plan a 3-minute worry break for later in the day.
5. Take an online course in "improving your self talk" to be more positive.
6. Resurrect an old interest (e.g., singing, bird watching, dancing, photography), and take a class to get back into it.
7. Take a walk at lunch time each day (in any kind of weather) to feel healthier and less stressed.
8. Begin each day with a half-hour of quiet reflection and goal setting.
9. Take the lead in planning a family or friends reunion.
10. Start a project or activity you've been meaning to do for years.
11. At the end of a busy week, watch a couple of comedies that you anticipate will make you laugh out loud.
12. Learn a technique ("change your thinking to change your feelings") to deal with your emotional reactions to unpleasant or upsetting events and improve your optimism.
13. Build a support team that will provide honest feedback in a supportive and positive manner.
14. Learn and implement a system to become more organized and less stressed.

PLAN FOR COMPASSIONATE ACTION

In the following pages, you can read some ideas for how you can bring more compassion to your everyday life—for yourself, your family, your workplace, your friendships, your community—and to the wider world if you are so motivated.

After reading through these ideas, take some time to brainstorm some ideas of your own. What will you do to bring more compassion to the world?

1. PAY IT FORWARD

The research around elevation and the potential to create a chain-reaction of compassion provides hope for the idea that in any community (and perhaps in the global community) we can unleash a revolution of compassion by "paying it forward," committing to act with compassion for anyone we happen to interact with throughout the day.

- While shopping at the market, for example, we might help someone unload the items from their basket or perhaps take a moment to talk with the cashier who has had to cope with a difficult customer.
- We may listen patiently to the technician at the dentist's office who is worried about an aging parent or a difficult teenager.
- While driving in traffic, we can make it a point to be especially considerate of other drivers, bicyclists, and pedestrians.
- If we are serving customers in a restaurant, a friendly attitude and willingness to be helpful (even with rude customers) can be the catalyst that influences those customers to act compassionately on their own.
- Attending a meeting at the office, we can be alert to those who are feeling ignored or bullied and provide encouragement or speak up against the bully.
- We can be compassionate in talking with telemarketers, caring for children, or talking to a homeless person on the street. The opportunities for such actions are endless.

2. TEACH AND LEARN COMPASSION

Scientific research into the measurable benefits of compassion indicates that individuals can benefit personally by learning to be more compassionate. Compassion training programs for adults are underway at several institutions including Stanford University, Emory University, and the University of California, Berkeley. While findings are still preliminary, the research suggests that compassion can be learned, that formal training can help, and also that being compassionate can improve health, well-being, and the quality of relationships.

The Greater Good Science Center at Berkeley indicates that many scientists believe that compassion may even be vital to the survival of our species. On the Greater Good website you can read about some of their research findings, which include benefits of compassion for the health and happiness of individuals, parents, spouses, friends, and employees.

Another useful tool for bringing people together is provided by the Compassionate Listening Project, a non-profit organization that offers the services of independent facilitators who offer training in their Compassionate Listening curriculum. They are dedicated "to empowering individuals and communities to transform conflict and strengthen cultures of peace."

Author Olivia McIvor, in her book *Turning Compassion into Action*, provides some practical suggestions for those who want to reach beyond themselves to develop their compassion. In discussing the sense of loneliness that seems to pervade everyday life in our technological society, McIvor asks, "What would compassion do?" to bridge the gap for individuals who are feeling lonely or isolated. She suggests:

- Create a new circle of friendship.
- Meet someone from another generation.

- Talk to a neighbor.
- Create or join a compassion club.
- Reach beyond your current boundaries.
- Identify what makes you feel included and forward that to someone else.
- Volunteer in your community.
- Commit to a conscious act of kindness every week.
- Ensure everyone feels valued, respected, and heard.
- Acknowledge someone you usually ignore.
- Ask, "What do you think?"
- Listen with love.

3. GAIN EMOTIONAL INTELLIGENCE SKILLS

The skills that contribute to the various components of emotional intelligence (often called EI, or EQ)—self-awareness, self-management, awareness of and interaction with others, and resilience—can provide an excellent foundation for community builders in their work to bring awareness, build empathy, and move people to compassionate action within their communities. Emotional intelligence can lead to the development of empathy and compassion.

One of the foundational aspects of Emotional Intelligence, for example, is self-awareness, which includes "emotional literacy," the ability to identify your feelings and emotions in a given moment so that you can then learn how to *manage* them. Emotional literacy, like other skills of emotional intelligence, can be taught and learned.

Empathy—the ability to recognize and identify with the emotions of others—is another significant aspect of emotional intelligence training. A well-developed sense of empathy, or "emotional resonance" with another, paves the way for the development of satisfying and productive relationships. It can also result in a greater understanding and a more compassionate view of all beings and their suffering.

4. BUILD COMPASSION EDUCATION IN THE SCHOOLS

We would be remiss by not mentioning the opportunity to look to the future by introducing compassion and related concepts early and often in schools. Fortunately, there are a number of projects and curricula in many countries that purport to do just that. The Charter for Compassion website includes a great many resources in this vein and also invites schools and institutions of higher learning to sign the Charter for Compassionate Schools.

5. JOIN EFFORTS WITH OTHERS IN A GLOBAL COMPASSION MOVEMENT

In the past fifty years or so, largely due to technology and new modes of transportation and communication, we have moved closer to the realization that we can no longer live in isolated communities, that we are indeed interconnected and interdependent.

As a species, we can build on and extend familial compassion to an extended or blended family, to friends, and perhaps to acquaintances who share our community (a neighborhood, a school or college, a town or city, a state or province, or even a country). Efforts to foster and build awareness, empathy, and compassion in our own communities may lead to efforts on a larger scale—toward the realization of a world of peaceful co-existence.

It is our task as members of the community to nurture those seeds of compassion in each other, so that they thrive, flourish, and make us capable of assisting all beings who are suffering or in pain in any way, both in our own communities and in every place on Earth.

WHAT STEPS WILL YOU TAKE? PLAN FOR COMPASSIONATE ACTION

Now it's your turn. Below are some suggestions for planning your own compassionate actions. Take some time to reflect, and then brainstorm about what you are willing and able to do in your own sphere right now.

1. Self-Compassion

Here are a few ideas. Are any of them right for you?

- Pat yourself on the back for your successes.
- Forgive yourself for mistakes.
- Learn your strengths and use them more.
- Enhance your Emotional Intelligence skills.
- Meditate and be mindfully present to each day and to every person you meet.
- Express gratitude.

What other ways can you think of to take care of yourself?

_____

_____

_____

_____

2. Compassion for Family and Friends

Here are a few ideas. Do any of them sound promising in your own situation?

- Use more active listening.
- Be aware of body language.
- Demonstrate genuine care and concern.
- Provide praise and encouragement—positive reinforcement.
- Be kind—in many ways.
- Respect privacy.

What other ways can you think of to increase your compassionate action with family members?

_____

_____

_____

_____

3. Enhancing Emotional Intelligence Skills

The premise of *Emotional Intelligence for a Compassionate World* is that the skills of Emotional Intelligence, which can be taught and learned, are essential for individuals who are working to make a positive impact--in themselves, in families, in the workplace, in the community, and in the world. Consider using the "Action Plan for Enhancing Emotional Intelligence," which is included in this book.

4. Compassion for Your Community

Here are a few ideas. Your community may be a small town or a huge city or somewhere in between those two. In any case, it will probably include both people you are at least acquainted with and many who are strangers.

- Get to know people who are "different" from you.
- Treat all people with respect.
- Be sensitive to body language and facial expressions.
- Express appreciation when someone acts with kindness.
- Listen actively and attentively to other points of view.
- Advocate for those who are unable to speak for themselves.
- Volunteer to help those who are suffering in some way.
- Speak and act mindfully.
- Smile at a stranger.
- Join with others to initiate a "compassionate community" within the <u>Charter for Compassion International.</u>

What other ways can you think of to take compassionate action in your community?

_____

_____

_____

_____

Appendix

Emotional and Social Intelligence: Selected Resources

Andersen, Peter A. *The Complete Idiot's Guide to Body Language* The appendix to the book includes a thorough list of websites, books, and articles related to body language

Barsade, Sigal G. "The Ripple Effect: Emotional Intelligence and its Influence on Group Behavior," *Administrative Science Quarterly*, Dec. 2002. The results of this research confirm that people do not live on emotional islands but, rather, that group members experience moods at work, these moods ripple out and, in the process, influence not only other group members' emotions but their group dynamics and individual cognitions, attitudes, and behaviors as well.

Caruso, David R., Brian Bienn, and Susan A. Kornacki, "Emotional Intelligence in the Workplace," in *Emotional Intelligence in Everyday Life*, eds. Joseph Ciarrochi, Joseph P. Forgas, and John D. Mayer (New York and Hove, Psychology Press, 2006). In this chapter, the authors provide a "story" of a new hire, his manager, his team leader, and the organization they work in to illustrate the importance of emotional intelligence. They also provide a synopsis of the research on emotional intelligence.

Christakis, Nicholas and J.H. Fowler. *Connected: The Surprising Power of Our Social Networks and How They Shape Our Lives* (Little Brown & Co., 2009). The authors (one a health care policy specialist, the other a systems and political scientist) compare topology (the hows of a given structure) across different social networks to better explain how participation and positioning enhances the effectiveness of an individual, and why the "whole" network is "greater than the sum of its parts."

Clemons, Hank. *Applying Emotional Intelligence: From Mail Room to Board Room* (HLC Group, Inc., 2008). Hank Clemons is founder and President of the Society of Emotional Intelligence – a nonprofit organization dedicated to bringing emotional intelligence into practice in all walks of life including schools, families, organizations, and communities.

Colapinto, John, "Brain Games: The Marco Polo of Neuroscience." *The New Yorker*, May 11, 2009. This is a fascinating profile of Dr. Vilayanur S. Ramachandran, an Indian-born behavioral neurologist who is the director of the Center for Brain and Cognition at U.C.S.D. He has a reputation among his peers for being able to solve some of the most mystifying riddles of neuroscience.

Cooper, Robert K., and Ayman Sawaf, *Executive EQ: Emotional Intelligence in Leadership and Organizations* (New York: Penguin Putnam, Inc., 1997). The authors organize their discussion around what they call the "four cornerstones of emotional intelligence:" emotional literacy, emotional fitness, emotional depth, and emotional alchemy. The book includes the "EQ Map Questionnaire" which can be self scored.

DeAngelis, Tori. "When Anger's a Plus," American Psychological Association, March 2003 *Monitor on Psychology*, Vol. 34, No. 3. Despite its mixed reputation, anger can play a constructive role at home, at work and in the national consciousness.

Ekman, Paul. *Emotions Revealed: Recognizing Faces and Feelings to Improve Communications and Emotional Life* (New York, Henry Holt and Company, 2003, 2007). Ekman, who has been studying emotions for over 40 years, says that "emotions determine the quality of your life," and he discusses four "essential skills": becoming more consciously aware of when you are becoming emotional, even before you speak or act, choosing how you behave when you are emotional so you achieve your goals without damaging other people, becoming more sensitive to how others are feeling, and carefully using the information you acquire about how others are feeling. He has a website with more information: www.paulekman.com.

Ekman, Paul, and The Dalai Lama. *Emotional Awareness: Overcoming the Obstacles to Psychological Balance and Compassion.* (New York: Henry Holt and Company, 2008). This is actually a consolidation of conversations between The Dalai Lama and Dr. Ekman. Although the format lacks coherence, the book is interesting for bringing together the perspectives of science and spirituality to understand the nature and quality of our emotional lives.

Emmerling, Robert J., and Daniel Goleman. "Emotional Intelligence: Issues and Common Misunderstandings." The Consortium for Research on Emotional Intelligence in Organizations Issues in EI; (www.eiconsortium.org), 2003.

Fredrickson, Barbara. *Positivity: Top Notch Research Reveals the Upward Spiral That Will Change Your Life* (Random House LLC, 2009). "Written by one of the most influential contributors to this new perspective in science, Positivity provides a wonderful synthesis of what positive psychology has accomplished in the first decade of its existence. It is full of deep insights about human behavior as well as useful suggestions for how to apply them in everyday life." (Mihaly Csikszentmihaly, Ph.D.)

Freedman, Joshua. "2010 Workplace Issues Report: What are the top issues in organizations today?" Feb 20, 2010. The findings in this white paper are the result of a survey exploring top issues as well as employee attitudes and the role of emotional intelligence in solving these key issues.

Gardener, Howard. *Frames of Mind: The Theory of Multiple Intelligences* (1983, 1993). Gardener's work helps explain how and why people learn in different ways and possess different skills and talents. Gardener discusses his idea that "intelligence" is actually made up of various intelligences, including interpersonal and intrapersonal—concepts directly related to emotional and social intelligence.

Goleman, Daniel. *A Force for Good: The Dalai Lama's Vision for Our World.* (New York: Random House, 2015). In this book, with the help of his longtime friend Daniel Goleman, the Dalai Lama explains how to turn our compassionate energy outward. *A Force for Good* combines the central concepts of the Dalai Lama, empirical evidence that supports them, and true stories of people who are putting ideas into action—showing how harnessing positive energies and directing them outward has lasting and meaningful effects.

Goleman, Daniel. *Social Intelligence: The Revolutionary New Science of Human Relationships* (New York: Random House, 2006). Goleman brought emotional intelligence to public attention with *Emotional Intelligence: Why It Can Matter More Than IQ* in 1995. This book is a companion piece to that earlier book, providing information about social neuroscience and the variety of brain cells that help explain the neural dynamics of human relationships.

Goleman, Daniel. *Working with Emotional Intelligence* (New York: Random House, 1998). Goleman demonstrates how important it is for leaders to understand "emotional contagion," and the idea that a leader can infect a group with a positive or negative emotion, "like spreading a virus among unknowing victims."

Goleman, Daniel, Richard Boyatzis, and Annie McKee. *Primal Leadership: Realizing the Power of Emotional Intelligence* (Boston, Harvard Business School Press, 2002). Goleman, along with researchers Boyatzis, and McKee discuss the neuroscientific links between organizational success or failure and "primal leadership." If a leader resonates energy and enthusiasm, an organization thrives; if a leader spreads negativity and dissonance, it flounders.

Hojat, M. "Ten Approaches for Enhancing Empathy in Health and Human Services Cultures." *Journal of Health and Human Services Administration*, 2009, Spring 31 (4), 412-50. Describes ten approaches for enhancing empathy in health care environment: improving interpersonal skills, audio or video taping of encounters with patients, exposure to role models, role playing, shadowing a patient, hospitalization experience, studying literature and the arts, improving narrative skills, theatrical performance, and Balint method.

Iacoboni, Marco. *Mirroring People: The New Science of How We Connect with* Others (Farrar, Straus and Giroux, 2008). Iacoboni is Associate Professor, Neuropsychiatric Institute and Director, Transcranial Magnetic Stimulation Lab, Ahmanson Lovelace Brain Mapping Center at the David Geffen School of Medicine at UCLA.

Kunhardt McGee Productions. (Video – six hours) *This Emotional Life: In Search of Ourselves . . . and Happiness*. NOVA/WGBH Science Unit and Vulcan Productions, Inc., 2009. "THIS EMOTIONAL LIFE explores ways we can improve our social relationships, learn to cope with problems like depression and anxiety, and become more positive and resilient individuals" (from DVD case). Visit www.pbs.org/thisemotionallife to find additional resources.

O'Boyle Jr., Ernest; and Ronald H. Humphrey, Jeffrey M. Pollack, Thomas H. Hawver and Paul A. Story. "The Relation between Emotional Intelligence and Job Performance: a Meta-Analysis." *Journal of Organizational Behavior* (July 2011). Published online (www.interscience.wiley.com). This is an academic article reporting on an analysis of studies related to emotional intelligence and job performance. The results support the overall validity of EI.

Paul, Annie Murphy. "Your Brain on Fiction," *New York Times* (March 17, 2012).

Rapson, Richard L., and Elaine Hatfield, John T. Cacioppo. *Emotional Contagion* (Cambridge University Press, 1993). The authors propose a simple mechanism to account for the process of contagion. They argue that people, in their everyday encounters, tend automatically and continuously to synchronize with the facial expressions, voices, postures, movements, and instrumental emotional behaviors of others.

Salovey, Peter, "Applied Emotional Intelligence: Regulating Emotions to Become Healthy, Wealthy, and Wise," in *Emotional Intelligence in Everyday Life*, eds. Joseph Ciarrochi, Joseph P. Forgas, and John D. Mayer (New York and Hove, Psychology Press, 2006). Salovey, one of the pioneers of emotional intelligence, focuses in this chapter on staying physically well and on making good financial decisions. He argues that the appropriate regulation of emotions is an important predictor of good health and a key to investing money wisely.

Seligman, Martin E.P. *Authentic Happiness : Using the New Positive Psychology to Realize Your Potential for Lasting Fulfillment* (New York, Simon and Schuster, Inc., 2002). The author, Director of the University of Pennsylvania Positive Psychology Center, writes, "Relieving the states that make life miserable... has made building the states that make life worth living less of a priority. The time has finally arrived for a science that seeks to understand positive emotion, build strength and virtue, and provide guideposts for finding what Aristotle called the `good life.' " There is an interesting website associated with this book and concept: www.authentichappiness.com.

Seligman, Martin E.P. *Learned Optimism: How to Change Your Mind and Your Life* (New York, Simon and Schuster, Inc., 2002). Dr. Seligman explains how to: recognize your "explanatory style" — what to say to yourself when you experience set-backs — and how it influences your life. Like *Authentic Happiness* (see above), this book is based in the positive psychology movement, which can perhaps be summarized by saying that it "[shifts] the profession's paradigm away from its narrow-minded focus on pathology, victimology, and mental illness to positive emotion, virtue and strength, and positive institutions."

Southwick, Steven M. and Dennis Charney. *Resilience: The Science of Mastering Life's Greatest Challenges* (Cambridge University Press, 2012). Written by experts in post-traumatic stress, this book provides a roadmap for overcoming the adversities we all face at some point in our lives.

Tarvis, Carol. *Anger: The Misunderstood Emotion* (Simon & Shuster, 1989). "This landmark book" (San Francisco Chronicle) dispels the common myths about the causes and uses of anger -- for example, that expressing anger is always good for you, that suppressing anger is always unhealthy, or that women have special "anger problems" that men do not. Dr. Carol Tavris expertly examines every facet of that fascinating emotion -- from genetics to stress to the rage for justice.

Tjan, Anthony K. "How Leaders Become Self-Aware," *Harvard Business Review*, HBR Blog Network, July 19, 2012. Tjan is a co-author of the book, *Heart, Smarts, Guts, and Luck*. He says that the one quality that trumps all, evident in virtually every great entrepreneur, manager, and leader, is self-awareness.

USEFUL ONLINE RESOURCES

Coutu, Diane, "How Resilience Works – Improvising Your Way Out of Trouble." Harvard Business Review, 8/26/2002. https://hbr.org/2002/05/how-resilience-works.

http://www.authentichappiness.com - Authentic Happiness has almost 700,000 registered users around the world. You are welcome to use all of the resources on this website for free.

http://ccare.stanford.edu/ -The Center for Compassion and Altruism Research and Education (CCARE) at Stanford University School of Medicine was founded in 2008 with the explicit goal of promoting, supporting, and conducting rigorous scientific studies of compassion and altruistic behavior.. To date, CCARE has collaborated with a number of prominent neuroscientists, behavioral scientists, geneticists and biomedical researchers to closely examine the physiological and psychological correlates of compassion and altruism.

https://www.charterforcompassion.org/charter Read the Charter for Compassion on the Charter for Compassion International website.

http://www.cio.com/article/facial-expressions-test Facial Expressions Test.

http://ctb.ku.edu/en/table-of-contents/spirituality-and-community-building/being-compassionate/main - "Being Compassionate," Section 2 of Chapter 28, Spirituality and Community Building, Community Tool Box, University of Kansas.

http://www.danielgoleman.info Website and blog of psychologist Daniel Goleman, Ph.D., author of the *New York Times* bestseller *Emotional Intelligence* and *Social Intelligence: The New Science of Human Relationships*.

http://www.eiconsortium.org - The mission of the EI Consortium is to advance research and practice of emotional and social intelligence in organizations through the generation and exchange of knowledge. The Consortium for Research on Emotional Intelligence in Organizations is currently made up of eight core members and 56 additional members who are individuals with a strong record of accomplishment as applied researchers in the field. There also are six organizational and corporate members. The Consortium was founded in the spring of 1996 with the support of the Fetzer Institute. Its initial mandate was to study all that is known about emotional intelligence in the workplace.

http://www.emotionalintelligenceinsights.com – Information and educational tools for learning about and enhancing Emotional Intelligence.

http://www.eqi.org/fw.htm - Contains a list of over 3000 English words to express feelings.

http://www.greatergood.berkeley.edu - The Greater Good Science Center studies the psychology, sociology, and neuroscience of well-being, and teaches skills that foster a thriving resilient, and compassionate society.

http://www.mindtools.com – "Active Listening: Hear What People are Really Saying."

www.nacada.ksu.edu/Resources/clearinghouse/View-Articles/body-speaks.aspx "Body Speaks: Body Language Around the World," Kris Rugsaken.

http://www.paulekman.com – Eminent psychologist Paul Ekman's site, which includes some brief videos on gestures, universal emotions, and learning to recognize microexpressions to read emotions.

http://www.thp.org/knowledge-center/know-your-world-facts-about-hunger-poverty/- The Hunger Project.

http://www.utne.com/Mind-Body/Finding-Happiness-Cultivating-Positive-Emotions-Psychology.aspx An interview with Barbara Fredrickson about the benefits of positive emotions.

YOUTUBE VIDEOS (IN ORDER OF APPEARANCE)

"Best Babies Laughing Video Compilation" https://www.youtube.com/watch?v=L49VXZwfup8

"T-Mobile Sing-along Trafalgar Square" https://www.youtube.com/watch?v=orukqxeWmM0

"Christian the Lion" https://www.youtube.com/watch?v=md2CW4qp9e8

"3 Things I Learned While My Plane Crashed" https://www.youtube.com/watch?v=8_zk2DpgLCs

"Historia de un letero" (Story of a Sign) https://www.youtube.com/watch?v=hMas8TjqeUQ

"Ron Gutman: The Hidden Power of Smiling TED Talk" https://www.ted.com/talks/ron_gutman_the_hidden_power_of_smiling

"Your Body Language Shapes Who You Are" https://www.ted.com/talks/amy_cuddy_your_body_language_shapes_who_you_are

"If We Could See Inside Others' Hearts" https://www.youtube.com/watch?v=Wl2_knlv_xw

"NOVA Science Now Mirror Neurons" https://www.youtube.com/watch?v=KA8xUayrLg

"CNN Hero Narayanan Krishnan" https://www.youtube.com/watch?v=y_3BEwpv0dM

"DeWitt Jones on Creativity" https://www.youtube.com/watch?v=tqF_D5GkrAo

"Louis Schwartzberg: Nature. Beauty. Gratitude." https://www.youtube.com/watch?v=8IXYZ6s3Dfk

About the Author

Barbara is the owner of Emotional Intelligence Insights, which offers online courses in Emotional Intelligence for leaders and others in the workplace. This book developed from an online course, *Emotional Intelligence for a Compassionate World*, offered by the Compassion Education Institute under the sponsorship of the Charter for Compassion. She has also created a computer-based game for teams, *Creating an Emotionally Intelligent World*, published by HRDQ.

In addition to earning her doctorate in English, Barbara has completed a post-graduate training course as a Master Certified Executive Coach and is a certified administrator of the EQ-i, an emotional intelligence inventory, as well as a number of other assessments to assist individuals, teams, and organizations in moving forward to fulfill their vision. She is also the author of *Letters to My Husband's Analyst*, *Read All Your Life: A Subject Guide to Fiction* and co-author of *You Can Choose Your Own Life* with psychologist Barry Sommer.

Made in the USA
Middletown, DE
11 September 2020